The Pay It Forward Series:

Notes To My Younger Self

Volume One

KEZIA LUCKETT

Published by Filament Publishing Ltd
16, Croydon Road, Beddington,
Croydon, Surrey CR0 4PA
www.filamentpublishing.com
+44 (0)20 8688 2598

The Pay it Forward series - Volume One
"Notes to my Younger Self" Kezia Luckett

© Kezia Luckett 2018

ISBN 978-1-912256-98-3

Printed by Ingram Spark

Dedication

Over the years I have been incredibly fortunate to have some strong female role models that have taught me what contribution is all about. Those close to home, like my mother who worked tirelessly every night to make the streets a safer place for teenagers to hang out, through to the women who came together from across the globe to share their stories in this book in the hope it would inspire other women and benefit hundreds more. To all of those women, I honour you for the work, dedication and contribution you make each and every day to making the world a better place.

To my loving husband Andy and our gorgeous children Amelie and Jack, thank you for your patience and understanding when I haven't been able to be as present in your lives during this busy period as I would have liked, you are my biggest supporters and I couldn't have done it all without you.

Contents

Your Turn To Pay It Forward

In your hands you hold a book containing a wealth
of knowledge, hope, wisdom and inspiration gained through
the experiences of life.

To truly understand the power of the written word and
what happens when women come together for a single cause,
read the stories within these pages and then pay forward the
knowledge to your girlfriends, sisters, mums, daughters, aunts
and to complete strangers who you believe need to read their
words to move from the dark times to the good and to know that
anything in life is possible

Write your messages of love, support, hope and inspiration
in the boxes as you join women from around the world in a
single cause because:

"United we are strong, Together we can make a difference, One woman at a time"

Pay it Forward Messages

To the woman you were, the woman you are and the woman you will be. Let your light shine for the world to see. Kezia x

Foreword

We've all asked the question "What if?"

What if I hadn't married my husband who was divorced with a child of 4.5 years and totally financially broke and had gotten together instead with a young judge from a rich family?

What if I had been born to a family that was rich and in harmony, rather than one where everyone was afraid of the abusive father and struggled with money constantly.

What if I had stayed being a lawyer and living in Belgium rather than becoming a Transformational Teacher that travelled the world?

What if I hadn't been so quick to make that decision?

Crossroads are an inevitable part of life, each situation offering us many different paths on which to travel. Like life, neither is black or white, right or wrong, feminine or masculine but a beautifully crafted, multi-faceted experience of contrast, allowing us to expand our souls, create new paths and increase our wealth of experience.

However, all too often on this so called "journey of life" we can experience those pivotal moments that can make us stop dead in our tracks, question absolutely everything and jet propel our life's trajectory in a completely different direction.

As I am sure you will appreciate as you start reading this wonderful collection of stories from key women of contribution from around the world, that the hindsight that comes with wisdom, age, knowledge and growth, allows us to see these moments of contrast for the pure gift from the universe that they are, however at the time they can often be enough to plunge us into darkness and possibly despair.

Looking over my life I have been gifted with many pivotal moments that have completely changed me. Some have been phenomenal like studying with the Spiritual Masters from seven years old, to saying "Yes" to appearing in a movie called "The Secret" that would ultimately go on to change millions of lives around the world, but with any contrast, there is always the other side. For me that contrast came in the form of a near death experience; a coma that would see me close to death's door. At the time as I lay in my hospital bed in recovery I became very angry. I had been a good girl and had religiously practised visualisation, affirmation and prayer and still…. here I was in a hospital bed with a multitude of health issues.

Looking back with the hindsight I have now, this pivotal moment was not only contributory to me realising my true gift as I discovered how "Bad Feng Shui" had seriously impacted upon my life but also moved me closer to connecting to my soul's purpose to enlighten more than 500 million people in the world.

This twisting, turning journey has allowed me to travel the globe helping millions and work with the very best companies, celebrities and people through my transformational work as a Feng Shui Master. As I have moved across the world I have always been inspired by the power of what happens when you bring women together with a collective goal. A mission so big it sometimes frightens them as they step up to improve the world and ultimately leave a huge, impactful footprint of contribution in their wake.

The Pay It Forward Series: Notes to My Younger Self book does just that, demonstrating beautifully what happens when women come together in collaboration not competition, in contribution not personal gain, with a real desire and passion to change the landscape of the world around them as they share those moments that many would like to leave behind, knowing full well that in the sharing of them others will benefit, others will feel empowered, others will believe and know that anything is possible, that their reality right now is not where their story ends but possibly a new beginning.

My hope for you as you work your way through the book, is that you too can gain the wisdom and knowledge in their words, in their heartfelt notes back to their younger self. That you gain the understanding that you too can pay it forward and that you will be joining millions of women all around the globe who are awakening to the fact that together we can change the world.

With Love   Marie Diamond
Global Transformaional Teacher, Speaker, Author and Feng Shui Master, star in the Secret.   www.mariediamond.com

Introduction

We all have those life changing moments in our lives, those times where you look back and know you have changed the course of your life.

Looking back over my life I have been fortunate to have had many. Some have been brilliant moments that have filled me with awe and lifted me into realms of happiness I could never imagine, others have seen me plunge into darkness where I have wondered whether I had it in me to come out the other side.

On a cold, wet, wintery Boxing day in England 2016 I had one of those moments. After spending Christmas overindulging, I got up before anyone in the house had started to stir, put my welly boots and wet weather jacket on, and braced the elements to clear my head.

As I started to walk an idea started to brew in my head, then suddenly an image appeared, quickly followed by another, and another. What initially started as a little niggle, within a few minutes became a barrage of information bombarding me every second.

I hurried home, sat at my computer and began to type. I began to ask numerous questions of myself as I tried to get to the bottom of the thoughts that filled my head.

Would life have been any different if I had been gifted with the wisdom I had now?

Would I have changed any part of my life to make it easier, less challenging?

What words of wisdom did I wish I had received as I navigated through life and would I have taken them if they had been offered?

As I began to ask questions, an idea of a book began to form. A book that would not only inspire, empower and lift the heart of the reader, but give back to women less fortunate as well.

With a clear picture in mind I contacted a few women I knew and talked about my idea. Word quickly spread and within the short space of a month not only had I started to receive stories from women around the world, momentum was building as the appreciation and benefit that writing a 'Note to your younger self' was felt.

My wish for you as you read this book is that you embrace the knowledge that you have, all the tools, strength and inner resources needed to walk your path on this journey of life.

Although hindsight is a wonderful tool, wisdom normally only comes with experience and many of us looking back would not change a single aspect of our lives, no matter what we have experienced as it has made us the women we are today.

I would like to say a massive thank you to all the amazing women who have gifted me, and the world, their stories and knowledge in this book in the hope it can inspire, guide and empower other women. I am truly humbled and thankful for your words that have forever touched my heart.

Enjoy the stories, take the wisdom that resonates within you, and if you feel moved to write your own "Note to your younger self" there is space at the back of the book to do so.

Lots of Love

Kezia xx

"**For a seed to achieve its greatest expression, it must come completely undone. The shell cracks, its insides come out and everything changes. To someone who doesn't understand growth, it would look like complete destruction.**"

-Cynthia Occelli-

Sticks and Stones Will Break Your Bones

Kezia Luckett, Positive Psychology Coach, International Speaker and the CEO & Trailblazer behind the Women of Contribution Movement.

What are you passionate about and how you are contributing to the world?

I believe that every woman on this planet can leave an impactful footprint on the world with the right support, resources and network, which is why I created the Women of Contribution movement; a place where women can honour, support and learn from one another.

Describe a pivotal time in your life that you wish to share.

I want to take you back to a time in my life where I thought life was not worth living. I would have been about 13 years of age and my parents had moved me from the thriving town of Brighton to a small hamlet in the middle of the countryside in Devon where I knew no-one and being different was not celebrated.

I had loved my previous home, my school, my friends but here I felt like an outsider. Looking back, I think that my father had just hit the so called 'midlife crisis' and believed that there had to be more to life than the corporate 9-5 job and was on a mission to move to the country, set up a business and live the 'good life'.

The reality was that move plunged us into financial instability. Not so many months after the move, and as my father was establishing his new business, the market took a downturn. What was once an opportunity of a lifetime would see us struggling to make ends meet, with fear and worry becoming a constant visitor at our home.

Starting a new school can always be a little difficult but even more so with teenage hormones raging through your body. As I tried to fit in, blend in and become invisible I inadvertently attracted the attention of bullies. There were three separate groups that made it their mission to make my life a living hell: the young girl who thought I fancied her boyfriend, the other outsider

13

whose skin colour made her stand out and whose bullying made sure no-one messed with her, and the friend who had for some reason flipped to enemy in a moment's notice.

As an adult I have spent many years looking back at this time with adult eyes and the foresight of experience and know on many levels I had my part to play in the situation. I had arrived at the school playing the part of 'Miss Confidence' whilst deep within I felt like wobbly jelly and have often wondered whether that mask of confidence could have been perceived as cockiness or a sense of thinking myself better than others.

Regardless of my part to play as the first punches landed, the taunting, disempowering words rang in my ears and the level of fear of going to school or being by myself increased as my self-esteem was gradually worn away, my self-worth smashed and I retreated further and further into myself until that happy-go-lucky, confident child seemed to disappear completely.

Looking back, what made it such an important part of your life journey?

The bullying truly shook me to my very core, its effects lasting for decades to come, but this was not the reason it is such an important part of my journey. Now that I can look back with the wisdom, knowledge, understanding and self-love I have now, I realise that those moments, those dark sometimes unbearable moments, taught me so many life lessons. At the time it felt like every day, every year, was consumed with bullying but in reality, these were just moments, small snippets in time, a story I would go on to tell for decades to come.

The reality is my perceived danger of constant bullying meant I lived most of my teenage years in fear. Fear of the bullying, fear of bringing attention to myself, fear of being me and not being liked for it.

In those moments of fear, I gave up control and allowed others to enter the sacred space of my mind, dictate and shape my destiny, my life, my reality. I not only allowed it, but started to use their words as my TRUTH, my STORY, my LIFE.

I became small, so small in fact it is only in my 45th year that I truly understand the impact of being small and playing small has on my life, my business, and my future.

I know now that our reality is what we make it. I didn't know at that time the power of my mind, quantum physics or universal laws, or how what we think, can become our reality. I thought only in terms of fear, therefore my mind, like Google, searched for images, words and videos associated with that term, constantly looking for things to be fearful of. It discarded the good times and only recalled the bad, it searched out those times in my internal database that matched its search criteria and I quickly became a pessimist about life, the future and the past.

But the experience of bullying was one of life's greatest gifts to me. It allowed me to expand and grow, to tap into my natural abilities, to recognise my self-worth, to not judge, to look at life from all perspectives, to realise that those doing the damage are often trying to escape their own pain.
It provided me resilience, hope in the face of adversity, and the drive and determination to get out of that place and explore the world and take my destiny into my own hands. It was instrumental in my move to leave home at 19, to travel, live, work and study in America by myself at 21 and try many different, new and exciting things without all-consuming levels of fear.

Based on the wealth of knowledge, wisdom and experience that you have now what would you have liked to say to yourself back then?

Dear Kezia,

As you fumble through each day with your head bowed down avoiding eye contact, you might find it hard to ever contemplate that life will be any different from where you are now. The daily drudge, the hiding, the trying to be invisible, but believe me when I tell you that you will reach a point where your life will improve beyond recognition and surpass even your wildest dreams so much so that you will often wonder why you cried so hard each and every day.

When you look in the mirror now you see a gawky, skinny, uncomfortable girl who, daily, hears the taunts of others as they make you believe that no one could ever find you attractive, that your body shape is something to

15

be ashamed of and covered up. That someone like YOU, should never have come to THEIR school, to THEIR area, or even dare to be in THEIR presence.

But please, during your delicate teenage years, don't start to look externally for approval and acceptance as you won't get it, because unbeknownst to you right now, all your peers are also struggling to find some form of understanding.
They too are searching for their rightful place in society and unfortunately, they haven't yet discovered that women, real women, support each other rather than tear each other down, collaborate rather than compete, recognise their true inner beauty rather than belittling others to feel good. My darling, beautiful girl, please note that in your search to find acceptance and assurance from others that you mustn't confuse sex with love or acceptance.

Look within to discover your true self-worth and accept your body for the healthy, flexible, strong, earthly home that it is. Please treat it with love. Honour it with the right food, know that it needs to be exercised, stretched, and pushed regularly to discover your limits and continue to work.

Don't drop your standards in order to fit in. Don't dumb down in school, don't hide your love of learning, don't be afraid to show your interest, to question "Why?" as those learnings just stimulate more questions and will make your mind explore possibilities that seem totally out of reach. Don't worry how your intelligence and interest will be perceived by others, they are on their journey and you are on yours.

Try everything!

Don't let fear get in your way, because often it is just your imagination playing tricks that there is something to be fearful of.

Grasp every opportunity that is presented to you with both hands and run with it, even if you don't know where it will take you.

Please, please don't believe that lack of money, the right accent, the right clothes or the right skills will stop you from becoming the inspirational, powerful woman you have always dreamt of. You will succeed in spite of *those things you consider to hold you back as you burst through all your preconceived barriers to follow your purpose and truly understand that there is nothing you cannot learn, do, or achieve if you set your mind to it. Know that when you finally step up, step in, and become visible in your authentic space and follow your soul's inner guidance, all the resources, connections, confidence and focus will become visible and will flow in abundance to you.*

For your peace of mind, please learn early on how to forgive others because holding on to this level of resentment, rage, sense of injustice and shame will not be healthy for you and could lead you to constantly feeling ill and lethargic.

Instead let the words and taunts of others roll off your shoulders, release their impression of your body as THEIR hang ups, rather than accepting it as your reality, otherwise it will haunt you and restrict you from trying new things over the next 25 years.

Practice the art of forgiveness often. Try to understand the situation that your abuser finds themselves in, bullying is a learned behaviour and normally says far more about the bully than the person being bullied.

Please know that with the bullying you endure, not only in your teenage years but later in the workplace, comes an inner strength. A resilience that will often make you feel invincible and help you to bounce back over the next 30 years of peaks and troughs of life, empowering you to adapt to any situation, increase your levels of hope and develop strengths that you could never, ever imagine holding.

With this strength and understanding will come a sense of empathy for others that will have people constantly questioning, "How do you always know just the right words to say to make me feel better?" This is one of your GIFTS, lavished on you in abundance but you must learn quickly how to use it wisely.

As you develop a drive and desire to make life better for everyone and anyone who crosses your path, especially women, you will feel to the very core of your being what injustice feels like which will often see you fight for the underdog and develop a real need to 'fix' or 'save' others that you view in pain.

" **Don't believe that lack of money, the right accent, the right clothes or the right skills will stop you from becoming the inspirational, powerful woman you have always dreamt of. You will succeed in spite of those things you consider to hold you back** "

-Kezia Luckett-

But, beautiful girl, please listen to these words carefully as you need to know this before you invest so much of yourself in others.

It is not your job to 'SAVE'.

That is their job. They have lessons that need to be learnt, to build their strength and determination to get back up after a fall, to grow and expand in the way their soul is meant to. You can only offer them a safe space to explore those inner feelings, release, and let go. Offer them support and provide them with the tools needed to move on from their pain and step out of the shadows as this is their journey and birth right.

Know that through the years when you look in the mirror and show disappointment that things didn't work out as you planned, you cannot judge your success by others or hold tightly to the outcome of the situation. Social media is a wonderful tool but not everything is always as it seems. It is often a place of smoke and mirrors, with many putting on the societal mask and stepping out on this stage called life and acting in the way they think they are meant to, but the only thing we are MEANT to do is live a life of happiness and fulfilment in our own way.

Just take note here: You are on your journey and you are right where you are meant to be, so please stop comparing yourself to others.

Embrace your life, every minute of it. Give glorious thanks to God for the wonderful women you will meet along the way, women who will inspire, women who will push you out of your comfort zone, women who will challenge you to think differently, act differently and help you to discover your authentic self. Please share this gift and pass it on to the other women who might cross your path.

You may at this moment in time think this will never happen, that life will never improve, but when you reach 45 years of age you will look back and strangely cherish the memories of the bullying you received in your teens as it made you the exceptional woman you are today.

Everything you have experienced in your life from the bullying, depression, heartaches, health problems, burnouts, miscarriages, general ups and downs, and all the good stuff in between, provide you growth, expand your soul, and although they don't define you, they do allow you to use these experiences to empower others as you continue on this journey called life.

Remember though, as you become successful everyone will have an opinion some will voice it loud and clear, they are the easy ones to deal with, the harder ones are the ones who keep quiet. Those who show no interest in your work or your mission, they are the ones who will prompt doubt and will often sit closest to you. But listen, and listen carefully; like the bullies, they are probably fighting their own demons, possibly those of insecurity and jealously. Know this, they will be removed as and when the time is right, allowing you once more to focus on your mission rather than why you don't feel supported, or feel betrayed.

One thing I need to say to you is going to seem strange, you are going to question why this is important, but it is. You know those images, words and questions that pop up from time to time? Start paying attention to those. Don't discard them as fleeting interruptions but explore them in all their glory. Some can be thrown out but some, like the ones that come on a cold Boxing Day morning in the pouring rain, will have special significance. It will see you be led to a mission that is bigger than anything you have encountered in your life up to now, to become an advocate for women.

To step up, step in and become visible as the voice for women. To encourage them that those stories that sometimes bring up feelings of guilt, shame and fear can provide hope, wisdom and inspiration. Everything that happens in your 45th year has divine intervention layered around it and if you just trust, you will start to see the magic come alive in ways you never dreamed or thought were possible.

So, today, as I write back to the frightened, scared shadow of a young woman, my younger self, I want you to know I am here for you. That you are more loved than you could ever imagine by so many. That you are so worthy of all the good things that will come your way.

That you can now release the tight burden of control that seems to overshadow your life and let go of the worry, because that worry is just restricting your beautiful, creative, imagination that on those brief

moments of respite and trust believes that life will turn out wonderfully, and anything and everything is possible.
And when you do that, when you release and let go.........it will become your reality.

Lots of love always,
Your biggest fan,
Kezia xx

What golden nuggets did you learn from this experience?

Individuals throughout your life will offer you their gifts of experience, words and opinions, but it is down to you whether or not you choose to accept them or return them to sender.

As my experience, knowledge and understanding has expanded, so did my selection process of what I allowed to enter into my sacred space—my mind. Guard your mind against those things that limit your possibilities and open it to those that will expand your opportunities.

Life is too short to hold grudges and people's perceptions of any given situation is always different based on our experience, knowledge and interactions, so forgive and release and let go of what doesn't serve you.

What would you tell other women who might be experiencing this in their lives?

The old saying 'sticks and stones will break your bones, but words will never hurt you' has obviously not endured the wrath of a bully in whatever form that appears in.

Don't let this become your norm. My parents always told me to back down from fights and walk away but that didn't help me. Tell someone that this is happening and stand up for what you believe in. The minute I started to fight back like my life depended on it was when it all stopped as there is nothing more frightening to a bully than the realisation that they no longer have CONTROL.

Physical violence is never the answer but keeping quiet does nobody any good. Nip it in the bud early on and if that cannot be done extract yourself out of the situation.

What are some of the things you would have changed about that situation if you could have?

I wish I had stood up for myself earlier, both at school and in the workplace, but I really wouldn't change a thing. This experience like so many others has moulded me, it is part of my story, my journey and I look back with a strange mix of sadness and compassion for the bullies and what must have been going on in their lives, their self-esteem and their minds to think that what they were doing was acceptable. They probably have no recollection of these events at all.

Any final words?

Release the fear, let go of the control, grab every opportunity, follow your heart and, most importantly, step up, step in & become visible as the wonderful, superb, authentic and sacred woman you are and remember to ask daily, "Why am I trying so hard to fit in, when I was born to stand out."

How can people get in touch with you and see the work you do?

www.womenofcontribution.com
Email:kezia@kezialuckett.com
Facebook: http://facebook.com/groups/womenofcontribution
LinkedIn: https://www.linkedin.com/in/kezialuckett/
Telephone: (+44) 07810517739

Shut up and Shut It Out

Sammy Blindell, a.k.a. The Brand Brains, CEO of How to Build a Brand.

What are you passionate about and how you are contributing to the world?

Over 16 years I've trained more than 100,000 entrepreneurs to brand, build and grow sustainable business legacies from their ideas. It's so rewarding to see the ripple effect of being part of that change. I've learned that the more I give, the more I receive, and the more I receive, the more I can give. My vision is to see millions of entrepreneurs giving more to the world, so I get to watch the ripple effects of that kindness as it reaches every person on the planet.

Describe a pivotal time in your life that you wish to share.

If you had been with me 24 hours before, you would have been standing 5,500 metres above sea level, high up in the San Diego mountains looking up at a 40-foot-high wooden pole with metal footholds all the way up it, like big, fat, oversized staples. There we were, twenty-four change-making entrepreneurs and a documentary film crew, standing in a clearing amongst hundreds of tall trees with the leader of this team-building playground.

While some people in our group scaled the pole with ease, I wasn't finding it so easy. As I stepped forward to take my turn, I publicly declared, "I'll be happy if I get half way up!"

As the park leader clipped my harness on, I looked up and prepared to take the first step. One step up, two, three, four... I'm about eight feet up in the air and my left foot slips, making me nervous. I start thinking, "Ouch, this metal is pushing my rings into my fingers. It's really painful." Five, six, seven steps... I'm reaching with my right foot this time, and I can't find the next metal grip. I start to panic and everyone on the ground is cheering me on to find my footing. I find it, but negative thoughts are taking over. "This mosquito oil is making my hands slip off the grips." I take one more step and totally freeze. I ask to come down. The group is cheering me on at the bottom, "Come on Sammy, just one more step!" The encouragement helps and I take one more step up to about 18 feet, but it's not enough. I think, "They are going to brand me a failure if I fall. I'd rather come down with dignity." As I let go of the pole, the park leader winches me down inch by painful inch and that's when it first hit me.

"A failure, that's what you are. Why didn't you go further? You knew you could have done it. You've done it many times before with Greg and the kids. What an idiot you are that you couldn't get to the top in front of all these global leaders." I felt sick. Physically I could have done it, so why didn't I do it? How embarrassing.

I watched as one of the ladies achieved it on her second attempt, and she had the greatest disadvantage of us all... She stopped growing at three feet eight inches tall when she was a child. She is smaller than my four-year-old niece, yet here she is at 62 years young, less than half my height, and the metal foot grips from one to the next were taller than her whole-body height. All I had to do was use my leg strength to push me up to that next grip, while she had to use her entire body to lift her whole weight up to the next level.

I sat at the picnic table watching her every triumph and felt elated for her as she reached the top. Within seconds I was consumed with shame and thought about going again. But no sooner had that thought gone through my head, than the leader said, "Time's up, let's get back to the cabin." I felt drained.

I tossed and turned all night. I thought I could bury it and put a brave face on the next day, but as I sat in the circle listening to everyone proudly sharing yesterday's achievements to the cameras, I felt like I was going to combust.

As they announced a quick break, Donna Tornillo, a powerhouse of the most incredible energy, came over and sat down next to me. "I've been told you need a hug, Sammy. Do you need a hug?" she said, as she nodded skywards to let me know she'd been given this divine appointment from a higher source. I buried my head in her shoulder and sobbed for ten minutes as she gently hugged me and stroked my back. After what seemed like a lifetime of tears, I finally found my voice to speak.

"I hate liars Donna", I said to her.

"Oh dear, who has lied to you?" she said with a concerned look on her face.

"I did. I lied to myself that I couldn't climb that pole yesterday. I lied to myself that my rings were hurting my hands too much to continue. I lied that the mosquito oil was too slippery. I lied that I was too fat to be up there. That I looked stupid. That it was okay to settle for half the success, but it's really not. I've never settled for anything less than 100%, so if I've lied to myself about this, what else am I lying to myself about?" I said.

As the words tumbled out of my mouth, I started to remember all the things in my life that I'd said no to, in case I failed. Opportunities I'd missed, because it's easier to say no than fail. Relationships I'd walked away from, before they could hurt me. Projects I'd turned down, because I wasn't enough. Parties I'd said no to, because I was too fat.

"It sounds to me like that pole needed to confront you yesterday, so you could have it out with yourself, Sammy", Donna said. I nodded in agreement and with that, she bent over, kissed me on the forehead and left me alone with my thoughts.

Wow, what a realisation! Being a failure was a lie I'd been telling myself for years, put in place by my ego to protect me from rejection. But that protection was holding me back from achieving so much more than I was capable of and forcing me to live a smaller life than I was put on this earth to experience. Now I was being totally honest with myself, it was glaringly obvious. I wouldn't put up with someone else lying to me like that, so why have I allowed myself to do it all this time?

As I pondered on this, a movie started playing in my mind of my first day of school. I was five years old, bouncing around like a flea with excitement and as we were let out into the playground for our first break, I ran over to a group of girls playing a skipping rope game in the playground. As I approached them, one girl put her hand up to my face, "Go play somewhere else fatso, you can't play with us."

I was devastated, and right up until this moment of clarity thirty-six years later, I hadn't made the connection. I let that girl brand me fat and I'd felt like a failure ever since, terrified of rejection. I've carried that label around my neck like an invisible logo for the rest of my life up until now. Isn't that interesting? Now it was clear to me why I fight so hard to stop people branding themselves with the wrong label and reputation. Now I know why community, inclusiveness and relationships are so important to me, causing me to build a global centre of excellence for entrepreneurs who want to feel safe and supported as they grow their businesses.

That girl at just five years old gave me an entire career and the gift of changing millions of lives by doing what I do now. I learned very early on in life that if you don't take control of your label, you are leaving your reputation on the table. If you don't believe in the brand you are building, nobody else will, and if you don't take control of how you see yourself, someone else will.

Based on the wealth of knowledge, wisdom and experience that you have now what would you have liked to say to yourself back then?

Dearest, brightest, beautiful Sammy,

You have enough love within you to love everybody in this world millions of times over. Your heart is pure and your soul will shine brightly in everything you do, because your lesson here this lifetime is to LOVE and BE LOVED.

You are blessed. Your entire life is going to be filled with the most beautiful, spiritually enlightened souls who will bless your every walk to keep you focused on what is true and real. Whenever you go off track, God will send earth angels at the right time, gifting you the lessons you need to receive and getting you back onto the right path for the walk you chose for this life.

There are going to be times when you don't learn the lessons straight away and it's going to hurt for a while. The more you avoid these lessons, the more painful it will be. The longer you hide from the truth, the longer the suffering will continue. The more you go through these experiences on your own, the greater the loneliness will become. But you will learn these lessons quickly and over time you will trust and allow without asking how. It's going to be easy to blame yourself and others for the pain. But please remember that it's not going to hurt for long and the lessons you learn from each experience will be valuable for you and others later on. You won't realise it as you are going through it, but you are going to take these lessons and support others to help them avoid taking that same painful path, transforming millions of lives and building a global movement in the process.

Sometimes you will go from making one mistake to another that hurts even more than the one before it. When you are buried inside a situation and fear kicks in, you will become temporarily paralysed and you won't always see the light that's awaiting you on the other side. But it really is only temporary, and God will always send you an earth angel to walk the path with you, supporting you through it and guiding you toward the light.

Just as paddling in a cold ocean is uncomfortable when you first step into it, the painful experiences coming up in your life won't be comfortable either. I promise you that you will adapt quickly to the temperature and you will be ready to go in further, normalising each step that takes you deeper. Just trust the process, fail fast, recover faster and trust that even when it feels like you are going under, you are in fact rising to a new level of consciousness, purifying and healing your spirit to create even greater experiences for yourself and others around you.

Sammy, everything is possible when you fully believe in yourself. It's when you finally realise you deserve love and to be loved that your life is going to become richer in every aspect of your existence. However, you are going to get half way through your life before you realise this.

One of your earliest lessons is when your biological father leaves for yet another conquest when you are just two years old. You will have very visual and painful memories for a long time of the things he said and did to both you and your mum in the short life you will have had up to that point. You will have already learned that to have an easy life, you just need to shut up and shut it out.

Whilst you and your mum move in with your grandparents to start your new life, you will develop a habit of comfort eating while your mum is at work. Your grandma gives you sweets, crisps, chocolate and fizzy drinks to fill the void of you missing your mum so much. You learn to distract yourself from pain by using food as a crutch. This keeps the anxiety and pain pushed deep down until she comes home again. You eventually trust she is not going to leave you too, but the belief that you are not worthy of your dad's love and that's why he left you leaves you with abandonment issues, fear of loss, separation anxiety, relationship challenges, emotional

"Just trust the process, fail fast, recover faster and trust that even when it feels like you are going under, you are in fact rising to a new level of consciousness, purifying and healing your spirit to create even greater experiences for yourself and others around you."

-Sammy Blindell-

eating problems and fracturing your trust of others for the next 37 years. Not everything around that time is going to be negative though. You will learn the power of healing, spirituality, integrity and generosity from your grandma. You will learn the power of innovation, technology, pride and dedication to your work from your Grandad. You will learn the power of creativity, tenacity, passion and community from your mum. And when she meets the real love of her life, Martin, just 18 months later, you will learn the power of commitment, loyalty, authenticity and family when he adopts you as his own daughter and you become best friends forever.

You will work hard and get head-hunted several times, enjoying a great career and plenty of material things that most people would be envious of before the age of thirty. However, the company you love working for will make some BIG mistakes and fold, leaving you without a job just before Christmas. Inevitably, Christmas is awful and you will put a smile on your face to let the rest of the world believe you are okay. But the pain of not being able to buy presents for everyone is going to stay with you for a long time.

You will take the first design job that comes your way just to get out of the house. It's a toxic husband and wife team that has an atmosphere you can cut with a knife. You get through the days by carrying your first mantra with you... 'shut up and shut it out.' You will hate working there and after nine months, they will close the business, nine days before Christmas. You will be out of work again.

You will learn so much about how not to build a business over the next two years and after freelancing in many different businesses, you will know the patterns that tell you whether companies are going to flourish or fall apart. You finally pluck the courage up to work for yourself and just three weeks before Christmas, on 5th December 2002, you will be out of work again, but this time it will be different!

This might be the third Christmas in a row that you have not had a job, but this time you will be fully in control and decide to start your own business. You will go networking for the first time and realise you are brilliant at connecting the right people together.

You will be scared to death at having to stand up in front of people and speak, yet you do it anyway and as a result, you build a solid reputation as the 'go-to' person in your industry.

At the same time as starting your first business, you will become incredibly curious about the brand behind the branding. You will want to know why some businesses are doing extremely well, while others are failing miserably. You will go to hundreds of events and watch how people present their brand, themselves, their body language, their pitches, their brand colours and their business cards. You will find the psychology behind all of this absolutely fascinating and survey thousands of business owners around the world to find out what's going on behind and beyond their brand. You will survey hundreds of customers to quiz them deeply about their experience and you will get qualifications in all the areas of buyer's behaviour, marketing, psychology and colour that will take you to that next level. As a result, you will develop intuitive skills that are spot on 100% of the time and business owners will travel from all over the world, paying you tons of money to get your advice on how to build their brand the right way first time.

Over the next seven years, you will launch another five companies with different business partners. You are going to learn some hard lessons during that time, but the greatest lesson of all is that money cannot buy your health back once it's gone. Fortunately, you will learn this lesson before it's too late, but only after ignoring how unwell you are feeling. Then one night, around 2am, you will have so much pain in your chest that you finally admit yourself to hospital. You'll be wired up to heart monitors three more times over the coming four months, but you won't tell anyone else about it. You'll just 'shut up and shut it out.' However, keeping all of this inside you will push you to breaking point and the fourth time you get admitted to hospital, the consultant will say, 'Ms Blindell, I cannot guarantee that what you are doing to your body is going to be reversible. You have to make changes now before it's too late."

You will take his advice seriously and after selling your business to recuperate in France for six months, you will fall in love with a house and live in France for the next four years. It's during that time, you start turning your knowledge into products and build a global resource for entrepreneurs of purpose-driven businesses. It will grow quickly, taking you all over the world, meeting the most incredible people. It's at an event you weren't even going to attend that you meet Greg, your future husband and loyal champion.

For the first time in your life, you will realise how it feels to be genuinely loved and supported. You will realise that everything happened the way it did for a reason and you will use that to take your next strategic steps with no baggage holding you back. You will come out of your chrysalis and it will be time to fly. It will be scary, but you will step into your new role as a wife and mother. You will become an in-demand speaker and coach on a global level, transforming millions of lives around the world and being financially recognised as one of the wealthiest women in the UK.

You will be wealthy in love, wealthy in family, wealthy in experience, wealthy in travel, wealthy in money, wealthy in legacy and most of all, wealthy in integrity.

xxx

What golden nuggets did you learn from this experience?

Going through this process now has been perfect timing. It has helped me to see that when I went through all those bad times before, I wasn't as emotionally equipped as I am now to get through the tough stuff. It took me three years to get the fire back in my belly before. Now it takes me three days. I am more resilient, more supported, more financially secure and more materialistically equipped than ever before.

I feel more love than I've ever felt before. I feel more supported than I've ever felt before. I feel God around me and inside me in a way I have never felt before.

I believe I have 100,000 angels by my side and they've got my back. I have more money coming in systematically than I've ever had before. I am traveling the world more than I've ever travelled before. I'm hanging around with people I would only have dreamed about being with before.
I am very lucky and forget that sometimes.

What are some of the things you would have changed about that situation if you could have?

I would be very protective of my time and stop saying yes to things that aren't serving my heart and others. I would value myself much more. I would care less about people judging me and care more about myself than others.

Any final words?

They say there are only two dates in your life that are important. The day you were born and the day you realise why you were born. I realised why I was born the day I was confronted by that pole and I'll be forever thankful to it for showing me what life is like without the weight of fear, judgement, and self-punishment holding me back. And I will also be forever thankful to that five-year-old girl for shaping me into who I am today.

My big takeaway from all of this is that you have a choice. You can choose to be fearful, or you can choose to be thankful. You can choose to fight, or you can choose to fly. And you can see your greatest obstacles as the very thing that's stopping you, or you can set a much bigger, scarier goal that makes your current obstacle look tiny in comparison.

Either way, it's your choice. Today is a new day and the first day of the rest of your life starts here. See you on the other side!

How can people get in touch with you and see the work you do?

www.howtobuildabrand.org
www.facebook.com/groups/howtobuildabrand

The "Realm of the Miraculous" Can Be Yours Today!

Barbara Brown, author, ordained minister, business woman, speaker, and wellness expert.

What are you passionate about and how you are contributing to the world?

I have been described as one of the world's most influential visionaries and change agents because I empower leaders to live in the "Realm of the Miraculous," pursue their highest purpose and fully enjoy their success. Over 32 years ago I was divinely healed of muscular dystrophy and today I direct leaders into victory through their own miraculous transformations with honest, open and authentic clarity from heaven's view.

I've been privileged to bring the Realm of the Miraculous to leaders in boardrooms and palaces and impart Whole Life and Whole Health as the guest of Kings and Presidents around the world.

Describe a pivotal time in your life you wish to share

MONDAY WAS FLAT-ON-MY-BACK TIME after another grueling week and a full day of church on Sunday. All of my muscles were exhausted...again. My legs wouldn't work, my neck wouldn't hold my head up, and my hands wouldn't grip. Nothing worked. The condition (muscular dystrophy), that I didn't want to acknowledge, was getting worse.

Lying in bed, I prayed, "God, I know You've called me to be a missionary, but how can I do it flat on my back?" (Women in the denomination I was in at the time could either tend the nursery at church, or go to Africa as missionaries.) Finally, I prayed a prayer God could answer, because my heart was to build his kingdom rather than mine.

I had become progressively weaker over the previous five years. The doctors at the Muscular Dystrophy Clinic in Little Rock, Arkansas, charted my decline by performing painful biopsies, shocking my nerve endings with electrodes, and slicing into my flesh to see how much muscle I had lost.

The diagnosis was Charcot-Marie-Tooth (CMT), the same diagnosis my dad received 33 years earlier. The doctors warned my family that CMT, a disease that causes progressive and severe muscle atrophy, was inherited and that two of Daddy's four kids would get it. The prognosis was grim at best.

"Someone has to know more," I told my doctor. "Where are the answers?" It wasn't okay with me to be crippled at only 35 years old. I had a life to live and my body needed to 'line up'. My last resort was to go to the MDA Research Center at Columbia Presbyterian Medical Center in New York City. Two weeks later, the doctor there confirmed the diagnosis I had dreaded:

"The tests are complete and they're all positive. You have Charcot-Marie-Tooth," the doctor said as he finished his analysis. "You know the progression of the disease. There's no treatment; there's no cure." I knew it well, having watched my dad and aunt both wither to death.

While the doctor was speaking, suddenly, JESUS APPEARED! I had no idea He made 'house calls' and I wanted to ask the doctor, "Do you have a clue who's here?" There was nothing in my data bank to prepare me for such a visitation.

Jesus looked down at me and said, "Barbara! When are you just going to trust Me?"

There was such life in His words that I stood up and declared to the doctor, "God's going to heal me! I'm going home. No more tests."

The doctor looked at me and laughed. I checked out of the hotel, headed back to Arkansas, and told my doctors there the same thing: "God's going to heal me! No more tests." They laughed too.

Two weeks later, I heard the Lord's voice say, "Start walking!"

"But God, this is killing me!" I replied.

He said, "You're dying anyway; just do what I said."
I began taking one painful step at a time...then five steps...then ten. At times, I was sure it would kill me. I walked and walked until, 30 days later, I RAN all the way home HEALED. Praise God!

Looking back, what made it such an important part of your life journey?

It never occurred to me to pray for myself, but for what I could contribute to fulfill the purpose for my life. I find today that when leaders give up their self-interest for God's purpose, they set in motion more than they ever dreamed possible as God builds, step-by-step, the life he has in mind. Some of the process may be painful, but it's worth every step to live in the Realm of the Miraculous where there's nothing as low as a problem!

Based on the wealth of knowledge, wisdom and experience that you have now what would you have liked to say to yourself back then?

Hey Little Girl!

There's coming a day when no one can tell you that cripples can't walk. You just stay focused on what God has put in your heart...That's the "what". Stay determined to fulfill the purpose and call He has upon your life...That's the "why". You don't have to know how He will accomplish His purpose in you...that's His job. But you know He can and you must believe that He will; meanwhile, like Jesus said, "Only believe."

No matter what friends, family, or doctors tell you, remember the scripture in Isaiah: "By his wounds we were healed." You know a God who's big enough to say the word and healing is inevitable and unstoppable.

You will know the One who said, "Let there be you," and He will become your best friend. He will remove the disease that threatens your life and he'll remove every trace from your children's DNA.

God will not only heal you, but He will free you to go wherever He sends you, with no thought about money or shelter.

You're destined to live in the Realm of the Miraculous and to share it

"I thank God for every situation, circumstance and relationship throughout my life. I may not have liked them at the time or want to volunteer for them again; however, apart from every step I took, I would not be who or where I am today, living in the peace and presence of God. "

-Barbara Brown-with leaders in high places all over the world. *From the madam in the whorehouse to the President in the White House, you'll know what it takes to live in the Realm of the Miraculous, and you'll know how to bring others there too.*

You'll learn to hear God's voice whispering inside you. More importantly, you'll learn to heed His voice and step out in faith to see things others can't, go where others fear, and say what others won't. As a result, God's power will work in the lives of those who touch yours, and those with ears to hear, eyes to see, and hearts to believe, will be transformed.

What golden nuggets did you learn from this experience?

It's exactly as Jesus said, "With man this is impossible, but not with God; all things are possible with God."

- God is bigger than any problem you think you have.
- If you ask Him, God always shows what I call, "His Strategy for the Victory."
- Where God calls you, there is grace to be.
- Any game is over when someone quits playing, and no one can make you play stupid games without your permission.
- Human nature drives, but God's spirit guides.
- Everything is a heart check.
- Obedience is always the dividing issue.
- God is always watching what we aren't.
- The hidden things always come to light.
- The cost is the call, or the call is the cost.
- If God calls you, He'll keep you, but if man calls you, you're bound and that's no place for a child of God to be.
- You and God are a majority.
- Living in the Realm of the Miraculous is not theoretical, but entirely practical and enormously satisfying.
- God is faithful.
- When God gets what He's after, you'll get what you're after.

What would you tell other women who might be experiencing this in their lives?

There may be no one in your world who sees who you are to God, or who supports your purpose, let alone shares it. You may never fit where others do or be satisfied to live in ways that others do. Jesus didn't either, so you're in good company.

If – and this is a big "IF" – you will turn your life over to Him; IF you will surrender your will to His; give up what you want for what He wants; then, and only then, He'll turn your tests into your testimony and you can find and fulfill the purpose for which you were created.

What are some of the things you would have changed about that situation if you could have?

I thank God for every situation, circumstance and relationship throughout my life. I may not have liked them at the time or want to volunteer for them again; however, apart from every step I took, I would not be who or where I am today, living in the peace and presence of God.

Any final words?

Read the book, the B.I.B.L.E., "Basic Instructions Before Leaving Earth," and do what it says. How will we pass this test called 'LIFE' if we haven't read the Book? By the time you've read from Genesis through Revelation twice, you won't have anything as low as a problem.

How can people get in touch with you and see the work you do?

Learn more at www.barbarabrown.com

Learning to Dance in the Rain

Ania Jeffries, founder of Women Work.

What are you passionate about and how you are contributing to the world?

My vision is to show the world that all is possible with the right mindset, community, network, self-belief and confidence. To Dream, Think and Play Big. My mission is to give women a voice, to inspire them to leave an impactful legacy for the next generation by growing new collaborations of powerful women who are passionate about empowering other women and the future generation.

Describe a pivotal time in your life you wish to share.

My pivotal experience was not just one experience. It was a culmination of four experiences that would actively change my life, force me to step out of my comfort zone, to look at myself in the mirror and ask myself who I was and more importantly, who I wanted to become for myself, my family and my children.

The Train Crash was the wake-up call. The shake-up of my world, of my haven of security, but also the foundation of a beautiful new beginning — of a new me. The realisation too that life throws unexpected challenges your way. You need to find the strength and the belief within yourself to know that you can and will survive.

The Redundancy was the reaffirmation that fear is a wonderful driver which pushes you out of your comfort zone to take the first step to create positive change in your life, to follow a path that you have been afraid to take because it means you have to take risks, to dip your toes into unknown waters, to find the guts to actually live your life the way you know you really should.

The Creation of Women Work was the realisation and the understanding that women are not invisible. We all have a voice which needs to be listened to and heard, and our children need to see and feel this too and learn that their voice is important. Each and every one of us has the power within to paint big, beautiful, colourful pictures in our lives, that is if we choose to. No one can make that decision for us. We are all strong, confident women who have the power to change the world and the world of the future generation.

An unexpected medical diagnosis was a reminder that one-minute life can be going swimmingly and then in the next breath it can be turned upside down, changed in a split second when you least expect it. Such experiences can push you to action your bucket list, to step away from Brian Tracy's 'Someday Isle', to motivate you to stop living in your shoebox of security, to cut some doors in the cardboard walls, to not be afraid to step through and experience a new adventure, one that you have been dreaming of for years. What's the worst that could happen? Nothing. As there is always a positive lesson in each and every one of these adventures. It's never failure. Always feedback.

Based on the wealth of knowledge, wisdom and experience that you have now what would you have liked to say to yourself back then?

Dear Ania,

Life is beautiful. You are 25 years old, you have a beautiful house, a gorgeous walled garden and the most amazing husband, who loves and adores you. You are newly married with a very supportive family (family means everything to you) and you also have the best job ever, you love it and you can't stop yourself from telling everyone it's your dream job. Life really couldn't be any better. But know that your life will change tomorrow, that something is going to happen that will completely change your life. Rest assured, it may take time for you to deal with it, but you will be ok. All will be ok. Accept that your life will take some adjustment, and how you deal with it will change you, allow you to grow new wings to fly, to follow your own dreams and, in turn, to inspire the lives of everyone around you.

On the 8 January 1991, a year before the birth of your first child, you will go to work as usual. You will walk fast down the hill wearing that big smile, excited about what the day will bring you at work. You will admire the beautiful oak trees along the busy main road with their different gorgeous shades of brown and will secretly express gratitude. As you stand on the platform huddled in your warm, winter coat you will watch the fellow passengers go about their daily business. I know how much you love to people watch. You will nod to those you recognise, exchange a quick hello, a smile, and step onto the train. To you it is going to be just another day, a very ordinary day, like any other.

You will find a seat on the train, sit yourself down and eagerly pick your book out of your bag to read. You can't wait to finish it. It's such a gripping story! The carriage will be busy and noisy with people jam packed in the aisles as the train fills up en-route to London. Occasionally you will look up, watch the other passengers or the scenery out of your window as the train thunders through the countryside and then allow your gaze to divert back to your book.

You will notice a father and daughter standing together in the aisle. The father will be trying to talk to her, to connect with her but she will not respond. She will just keep biting back with her quick, sharp, loud tongue. Pushing him away, humiliating him in your eyes, being so unkind. It will make you think of your own relationship with your father, how much you love him and how you would never dream of behaving in such a disrespectful way. You will just sit and stare, stare at them both. You won't be able to help yourself. You will become angry inside with the way she is talking to him and you will want to stand up and tell her to stop, stop her embarrassing him so publicly.

But you will be unable to as suddenly you will hear the screeches of brakes as the train overruns the terminus and crashes into the buffers of Cannon Street Station. You will be in the carriage that concertinas. You will be thrown across the carriage. You will remember a silence, an empty, eerie silence and then you will hear the long groans, the screams, those loud, unforgettable screams from the passengers, especially those from the daughter shouting, sobbing, "Daddy, I love you." Daddy will be crushed under the luggage rack on the floor, motionless, completely still.

There will be hundreds of injuries. People will die in your carriage. When you come around you will have no idea where you are, what has happened to you, who you are. You will find yourself in a complete state of shock. You will feel yourself floating as if you are an outsider looking in. The carriage will be filled with thick grey smoke. And through this smoke two firemen, two strong knights in shining armour, will come to rescue you, to carry you out of the train through the window.

And then you will see passengers stumbling, wandering aimlessly around the station, lying, crying on the cold ground of the platform, frightened, with blood pouring down their faces. People covered in bandages, being tended to by the ambulance services. You will just think of calling your husband, of getting to work, of continuing as normal. And then your husband, having heard about the crash on the radio, will arrive at the station to protect you, to look after you before you head to the hospital. You will be scared, you will have no idea what's going on.

But remember you will survive, you will be ok. You will keep asking yourself time and time again, did 'Daddy' survive? You will think if he did then his daughter would be able to apologise, she could make everything ok again between them and you could stop thinking about it. If he hadn't survived, that would be her last living memory of him. And you will continue to ask yourself this same question over and over again for many years to come, if not until you die.

Know too that your family, as much as you love them, will find it difficult to help you through this trauma. Again, not because they don't understand but because you will not allow them to. Know they will always be there for you and will be feeling helpless too. You will find real inner strength to deal with all the emotions that fill your head and your coping mechanism, your refuge, will be your garden. You will have the most beautiful garden in Kent but in the process of living behind a mask, wearing that smile for everyone to see, you will be dealing daily with the pain of this tragedy, trying to be strong for everyone around you because that is what you have always been told to do. That's what your parents have always done. Your father was a prisoner of war. He always taught you to be strong. To never show weakness.

You will shut down on people around you. You will close in on yourself and there will come a point when you will be unable to even open letters relating to your legal case of suing British Rail. The white and brown envelopes will gently drop through the letterbox onto your polished, oak floor. You will not want to pick them up to open them and as time goes on, as years fly by in the legal process, you will look at them, step over them and walk out to your beautiful garden. The letters will come fast and furious during the eight years, especially in the last few years it takes to sue British Rail. The sight of them will make you feel physically sick, afraid, tearful. You won't even want to touch them

It will be your husband, your rock, who will recognise your pain, who will take over. He will want to remove those feelings of helplessness that you are experiencing, and you will be cross with him because he doesn't understand your pain in the way you want him to, not because he is not a wonderfully kind man (it was one of the biggest traits that attracted you to him) but because you will not want to show him that you cannot deal with this on your own. You are recently married, and you will want him to only think you are strong. Not weak. It will be a challenging journey but know that you will get through this with the love of your family, that it will grow you and make you more resilient.

It will also be the unwavering support from your two bosses who will give you the belief and confidence that all will be ok, that all is possible. Both Peter and Gary will watch over you, will continuously challenge you to never give up on those dreams of yours.

These experiences will be the reasons why you decide to become a Life Coach and NLP Practitioner in later years because you will recognise that words expressed in haste without thought can be cruel or kind, can destroy or build you, and if you do not have the opportunity to make things right again, those last moments will live with you forever.

Know too that this will be one of four moments in your life, each of which will contribute to you being the person you are today. Four moments that will help you deal with fear. Four moments that will show you how capable you are of turning your life around, of showing courage, being adaptable to face all obstacles head on. You will decide to not allow these moments to define the woman you want to become, the woman you are today.

Each and everyone one of these will grow you, challenge you and allow you to be the voice you want to be in the future for so many other women and especially for your children. You will want to help women, young adults who have become invisible through personal life struggles, who no longer have the belief and confidence that they can be someone great. You will encourage them to find their inner sparkle, to love themselves again, to show their true vulnerability and beauty unashamedly to everyone whose lives they touch, to help them reconnect with themselves and bring enjoyment back to their own lives and to their families.

The next moment of fear, will come when your husband is made redundant when two of your children are at private school, and one at university. You will never forget the moment he comes home with the biggest smile on his face, delighted, thrilled to no longer be part of the banking world and all you will feel is fear, massive fear that your life is about to change, realisation that you do not want it to. This change will be a challenging one. You will have talked about it for years with family and friends, you will have discussed exit strategies, but you are not prepared when it comes. In truth you probably never would be.

You never really thought it would happen so soon. You will call one of your closest friends from the safety of your bedroom, where no kids can hear you and you will sob, shed those tears of fear and your friend, Andrea, will simply say to you, "You are one of the strongest women I know, and you will turn this into something very positive." You will always be grateful to her for those words (she will have no idea how much they were needed). You will pick yourself up and you will just focus on what you need to do, to show the family that this is a great opportunity to be following your passions and not just surviving to pay the bills, the lifestyle you have been living. You will make the decision with your husband to not return to the city but to join a franchise.
You will downsize in order to grow several new businesses. You will ask yourself if your friends will judge you, view you differently, and you will recognise quickly those friends who do support you. They will be the ones who will create true meaning in your life.

The hardest moment for you will be to recognise that you have not really given full gratitude to your wonderful husband (this will be the biggest eye opener for you because you thought you always had), to the 30 years he had worked in the city to support you and your family to give you all the lives that he so wanted and felt you all deserved, and that moment of realising how selfish you have been, with him getting up every morning at 4.30am and returning home at the earliest 7.00pm so that you could all live a beautiful lifestyle.

This will be a real turning point for you, to step up and put the self-pity aside. You will give thanks to the fact that the universe has given you an opportunity of growth, of transformation. The change will be a big one for both of you and you will all embark on a greater new journey of self-discovery, new creativity (neither one of you realised how creative you could be) where your wings will spread wider and bigger for the first time in years. And most wondrous of all, you will wish this change had happened sooner.

This transition will bring beauty to you all. You will move to live closer to your twin sister, your family will spend more time together and your children will find greater purpose, drive and determination to follow their own dreams too. Your son, Ben, will set up a successful digital marketing agency, www.influencer.uk your middle daughter, Emilia, will work at a company she has dreamt about working for since the age of 14, and your eldest daughter, Anousha, will move to Chile to pursue a new career—her love of travel.

You will realise that although you were happy living in that huge house of yours, you had become so stuck, scared to step out of your comfort zone, so complacent. You had been privileged and thankful to be able to stay at home with your children when they were small. You had loved every second, but you were not really growing and leaving an impactful footprint on the world, a legacy for your children, your husband, your family to remember you by when you are no longer on this earth. You will ask yourself the question 'if you were to drop down dead right now what difference would you have made to this world". That question will become your driver, contributing to huge moments of self-reflection. Your new life from this point on would be all about living with greater purpose.

You will meet a well-known motivational speaker, Kriss Akabusi, who will present you with a light-bulb moment at a workshop, one you never wanted to attend, one you thought would be boring and had to be dragged along to. You will be listening to him talking about Dreaming and Thinking Big and then suddenly, you will want to jump with joy and throw your arms in the air. You will run up to him at the end of the workshop and tell him that he has given you the belief that you can achieve absolutely anything in life you want, and he will help you to take the next step to achieve your

"Life is a gift from the universe. Sometimes you may not at first understand the situations that are thrown at you. You may initially immerse yourself in the negative but know that there will always be a wonderful message within. Just look for it. "

-Ania Jeffries-

dreams. He will become a great mentor to you, always there as a sounding board whenever you need to run through your ideas. The idea of Women Work will be born.

It will be your first event empowering women, leading women to a brighter future, encouraging them to believe in themselves, to be positive role models to their children. In just over five months it will snowball from a workshop of 20 people into a footfall of over 1300 with 51 speakers and 70 workshops, and it will bring you your third moment of overwhelm as you realise the full impact of your project on the community and everyone who is involved.

You will witness, first hand, women who truly believe in collaboration and not in competition and this realisation will drive you further to search out and work with true women of contribution. For you, these will be the women who will leave a footprint in the world you want to create for yourself, for your own children.

You will connect with the community in a way that you have never connected before and you will meet inspirational, beautiful women, mums who share your vision of wanting to make a difference in this world.

Working into the early hours of the morning to make this all happen, watching your son focus on his own future vision, your hubbie's drive to build successful businesses will become your driver. Because you know that if you fail you will show your children, your family, that it's ok to give up when the going gets tough. Your children will learn to stand on their own two feet, to deal with whatever life throws at them and, most importantly, to follow their own dreams. You turned this event into a success, a business that will be key to their personal visions of Dreaming Big and you cannot shatter that belief. You will show them that all is possible. And you will turn this event into a business with a team of wonderful like-minded women.

The next moment of fear will come when you are flying high after the huge success of Women Work. You will be so happy, ecstatic, walking on air, embracing so many new wonderful opportunities which hardly seemed possible before your husband becomes unwell and is diagnosed with blood clots on his thighs and pulmonary embolisms on his lungs. That moment *when you are sat with your rock, your baby rhino, when the doctor tells Simon that he should be dead, that he has no idea why or how he survived, will throw you back to that moment of fear, of fog, to the train crash in 1991 when you were closed in the carriage, unable to breathe, were suffocating. To that moment when you wanted to run and hide but you couldn't even find the strength to stand up.*

All those nights you will spend listening to your husband breathe, with your head against his chest, wanting to know he is safe, will just make you realise that you need to reframe your thinking again. You will recognise that your husband has been saved for a purpose (as you believe you were after the train crash) and he will give others the strength to overcome their own challenges and recognise that life is for living now, not for a tomorrow that may never come.

Know that it will also be that fear and your adaptability to reframe negatives into positives that will remind you of how much you want to continue to make a difference in this world, especially to your children, their friends, the next generation, and how much you need to live each second, each minute, each hour as if it is your last. To be grateful for what you have and who you have in your life. It is not the material possessions that define you but the memories that you create and the strength that you pull from each and every moment of your life, no matter whether good or bad.

You will win an award, The Coaching Academy Coach within Education Award 2017 in recognition of your life purpose and The Female Entrepreneurs Adventure Expedition will also be born, scheduled to take place in Malawi, October 2018. Your passion to inspire other women to make a difference in this world will continue with this expedition, which will be one of many. This will be just the beginning of a New You, the birth of new collaborations and partnerships, friendships and communities. Your father's words will always ring in your ears until you die, at every moment of fear, uncertainty, challenge, "Your past is not your future". You will keep reminding yourself to not be defined by what has happened to you but by what you can create and leave behind for the next generation. You will learn it is always important to ask for help, even when you are scared to, to not be afraid. To simply be authentic, to be 'you', your truth. Be the best you can and can give of yourself, and if others do not connect with you, it is not personal. They are simply not part of your future, of your journey. Your story will empower others to tell theirs too, to find their voice.

Just know that you are not alone. That beauty comes from each moment of darkness. Whether you choose to see the light depends on your mindset and only you have the strength to find the light at the end of every tunnel and you can find it. Never doubt that. Each and every one of us is here to support and grow each other. So, remember to be always kind to yourself, to self-care, to love yourself and forgive yourself too. None of us is perfect.

What golden nuggets did you learn from this experience?

Each and every one of these pivotal experiences brought new emotions into my life, wonderful golden nuggets of self-reflection, and personal and professional growth.

The Train Crash evoked huge emotions of fear and insecurity making me realise that no matter how much others loved me and wanted to protect me, they couldn't always make everything ok. This was a situation where I would have to find my own inner strength to move forwards. My family are at the hub of all I do and are always in the background to support me. I appreciate daily how lucky I am to have such support from my husband (the best rock ever), my children, our family. My twin (my other rock) lives in the same town as me. One brother lives fairly close by, the other abroad and, despite our differences sometimes, we are a close family. Distance creates no boundaries. I also understand how many do not have this network and I guess, deep down, this is why everything I now do, given my own personal journey, is focused on creating new networks of support and collaboration within the community for others.

Redundancy made me realise too that life is a choice of either fight or flight. I had a choice to either embrace the change that was hitting me/us as a family head on, fast and furious, like a brick wall or to just fight this change. It was going to happen regardless, and I couldn't stop it. I needed to show my kids that change happens every day. Do not fear it. Just embrace it. It is a wonderful opportunity to step out of your comfort zone and do something new, to grow in greater self-belief and confidence. I also learnt, most importantly, to be thankful for the opportunity of being offered a new lease of life whilst I had the energy to grab it. I still put out my gratitude to the universe on this front. At least now I can never say, "What if?" I chose to shut off the closed mindset (which I never thought I had!) and instead chose to adopt a 'bring it on' mentality which is a far more exciting, adventurous way to view the world.

Women Work opened my eyes to the fact that, as a mum, I had always believed that my role was to inspire my kids. Our children taught me that, in fact, they inspire me every day to Dream, Think and Play Big. To know and to truly believe that all is possible and that by following your own dreams you, in turn, inspire your kids and their friends to believe they can too. Some incredible women become invisible through the process of motherhood through no fault of their own and find it hard to get back on track and rebuild their confidence, their lives, new careers, and businesses.

They need to know they can get right back on track if they change their mindset and ask for help. The first step is always the hardest. I learnt that if you don't have the right support and network at home you need to find it in your friends, your colleagues, your community. Women Work brought this support to the community. Each and every one of us can achieve greatness and we, as women, need to work in collaboration and not competition to change the world for the better for our children.

An unexpected family medical diagnosis was another reality check that I had already lived half my life. It takes a challenge for you to really understand what this means. One moment life is great and then it can change in a split second, in a breath. We forget very easily to self-care (I still need to remind myself of this often and I need to). We all need to hit the pause button and stop running on that treadmill. Stop talking and dreaming about doing stuff and actually do it! Otherwise, you will still be having that same conversation with yourself in 5 or 10 years' time. Nothing will have changed, and in the process, you will never inspire others, especially your kids and your family to follow their dreams.

What would you tell other women who are experiencing this in their lifetime:

Reflecting on all that life has thrown at me over the last years I would say never be afraid. It serves no purpose and will not help you. Just know that whatever life brings to you, it is what the universe has decided for you. Do not fight it, find the beauty within it and if you cannot, then ask others for help, always.

Never, never, never give up.

Look forwards, never backwards. The only difference between an old and a new attitude is perception. So, change your attitude and, in turn, you will change your perception.

Life is a gift from the universe. Sometimes you may not at first understand the situations that are thrown at you. You may initially immerse yourself in the negative but know that there will always be a wonderful message within. Just look for it. Reframe your thoughts. Simply focus on the now. Be kind, be grateful and repay the gratitude. Pay it forward.

Find some tools or strategies to help you deal with stress whether it's meditation, lighting a candle, having flowers in your house, walking, sitting and breathing in nature. Find a mantra that works for you to help you through the difficult times. I always say to myself in a moment of overwhelm, "I can do this." And I always can. And if I need to, I always ask for help. There is no more hesitation here.

Don't sweat the small stuff either. It's a complete waste of your energy and your time, and when you look back on this period in time you will think it pointless. Instead, show gratitude for what you have been given, even in the deepest, darkest moments. This will help you through the darkness into the light, to allow you to live the life you deserve.

Share what you have learnt with others. Someone may need to hear your words. Surround yourself with women who believe in you, who will always be there for you through thick and thin, not just for the now.

Be true to yourself always. Know that you are beautiful. Say this to yourself every day and really mean it because until you believe it no one else will see the beauty within you. Above all do not be scared to show your vulnerability, never be ashamed. Just be authentic and you will become the brightest star in the sky. You may not always reach for the moon but know that you will always fall amongst the shining stars.

What are so me of the things you would have changed about that situation if you could have?

I would have shared my emotions with others, expressed my fears earlier, asked for help sooner and not felt that these were moments of weakness because I now know that they were moments of huge strength. I could have spared myself so much pain in the process.

I wish too that I had taken more time to reflect on my own behaviour and language and on the impact, it had on others when I would say stuff without really thinking about the consequences for others. I now realise, having qualified as an NLP Practitioner and Coach, having witnessed that scene on the train, that I fully understand how powerful words and actions can build or destroy. I think we should all think on this one more, especially if we are wanting to inspire others to be positive role models. I do every day. And I still need reminding.

Any Final words:

Always surround yourself with beauty, inspiration, and empowerment. Know that you are never alone. There will always be someone who will hold your hand and guide you. You will always find beauty from each moment of darkness. Whether you choose to see the light depends on your mindset, the people you surround yourself with and only you have the strength within you to find the sunshine at the end of the tunnel. You are here to support, grow, and empower others.

You are unique. You have been given the gift of life and the opportunity to leave an impactful footprint on this world, so do not waste it. Live each day to the fullest, inspire and build confidence in others and never let your candle burn out. Remember to be always kind to yourself, love yourself and forgive yourself too. Remember to be kind to others, to love others and forgive others too. They are on their own journey which has nothing to do with yours. Find your passion, follow it, and then you will find your purpose.

How can people get in touch with you and see the work you do?

www.nextstepmentor.com
Email: nextstepmentor123@gmail.com
LinkedIn: Ania Makowska Jeffries
Twitter: JeffriesAnia
Facebook: Nextstepmentor123
Instagram: Nextstepmentor123

Living the Love Code

I'm Danielle Morrow, speaker, author and catalyst for living a life you love, your way.

What are you passionate about and how you are contributing to the world?

I help people live a life they love, their way, by combining my extensive research, own personal life experience and an engineer's mind to simplify personal transformation into a LOVE CODE, that helps people break out from where they've been stuck, so that they can feel on fire, unstoppable and start living a life they love - authentic to them.

I am driven to help people love themselves, others, and their lives to heal the world and create world peace. By loving yourself and connecting with your divine self, suffering begins to disappear. My vision is that everyone gets to experience deep love in their lives and from there I see a world where everyone has access to clean water, air, and food, and we all lift each other up, support each other, empower each other, and we live as one.

Describe a pivotal time in your life that you would like to share.

Have you ever gone along like normal and then suddenly you just stop, take a look around and think, "I've worked so hard to get here and this isn't even what I want anymore. And frankly I don't even know what it is I DO want!"

You're burnt out and empty, now what?

My parents got divorced when I was six. Later in life, I realised that I had interpreted this to mean that I had to take care of myself. My father got custody of all five children so, while we had visitation with my mother on the weekends, I grew up in a single parent home. We grew up poor, sometimes on food stamps and sometimes wondering if there would ever be food in the fridge again.

I was programmed from a very early age that I had to work hard for everything. We grew up in a very chaotic environment which lacked structure as my father let us do pretty much anything. I was forced to become an adult early on and, as a result, I became determined not to repeat these family patterns, not to ever live in that kind of struggle again, so I developed this unstoppable drive and determination to become successful.

As a child it started with doing chores around the house, cutting coupons for grocery shopping, and pretty much anything else to get an allowance. I got a job the day I turned 16 to begin making money while getting straight A's in school and playing sports.

I am child number 4 out of 5, and I was the first one to graduate from high school and go to college. I had an inner burning desire to be successful and make money, and while focusing on school and sports gave me structure and a feeling of belonging to something, the home I lived in lacked love, affection, and warmth. It felt empty and barren of all those things that I believed would create a loving and comfortable environment. From this, I believed I was unloved growing up.

At school I excelled in maths and science, I went to college at 17, getting a degree in Electrical Engineering. I always loved maths and figured that Engineering would be a good career where I could make money and become successful. After college, I got a job as a software engineer, writing code for a living.

Around this time, I met a couple of patent attorneys which triggered my imagination as to what else could be possible; being a patent lawyer came with lots of perks including more money, so I went to law school in the evenings while working full-time as a software engineer.

It was hard going but eventually I got a job as a law clerk at a big law firm even before graduating law school. This was my life: I'd work all day, then in the evenings go to class for three hours, head home at around 10pm and attempt to read case law for 2-3 hours, preparing for classes the next evening. This went on for three and a half years, including summers.

Adding to this already exhausting lifestyle, the attorney training me at the law firm where I worked did not treat me well. I was so intimidated and young.

I didn't speak up or express my needs as I was overcome with fear, also I was still recovering from having lost my older brother who'd just passed away, so it was all I could do to even show up in the first place.

I remember walking into that high-rise building and before I even got to the elevators that took me to the 23rd floor where the office was located I could feel anxiety causing my entire body to contract and tense up. I would think to myself, "I have to spend another day in this office?"

My anxiety started to turn into physical symptoms. Sometimes I felt like I was going to fall over as I'd get on that elevator for another day with my equilibrium completely off.

I consulted with various medical doctors because I thought something was seriously wrong with me. However, they all said I was perfectly healthy. I refused to believe it, knowing something must be wrong with me as I could barely function. I told a friend of mine what was happening, and she told me it was anxiety and I should visit her psychiatrist and take anxiety medication.

Given I have always been anti-pharmaceutical, there was no way I was going to take anxiety medication, but it got so bad I felt like I was left with two choices: take the medication or quit my job and drop out of law school. I just couldn't go on living like this. I contemplated both for some time. Finally, one day, I couldn't take it anymore and gave my friend's psychiatrist a call. She didn't answer so I left a message and simply said, "I need anxiety medication, please call me back."

The psychiatrist and I played phone tag for three weeks. During that time, around Christmas, I remember shopping at Whole Foods and seeing a calendar from Wayne Dyer's 'Change Your Thoughts, Change Your Life'. As I stood and looked at the calendar it was like time stopped, the world stopped spinning and a laser light of focus zoomed in on the back of the calendar, feeling like some hidden treasure I'd just found, I held it in awe. I felt so connected with the translated versus written on each month of that calendar. I almost started to cry in Whole Foods. I immediately bought the calendar and went home, eagerly taking in a year's worth of monthly messages in one night. I balled my eyes out as I read the words in the calendar.

I felt so connected to my authentic truth/divine self and knew in that moment that there was a power and energy force greater than myself.

Synchronistically, the next day I went to work, there was a Barnes and Noble gift card as a Christmas gift from a co-worker on my desk. A light bulb went off in my head and I knew I had to go straight back to buy Wayne Dyer's 'Change Your Thoughts, Change Your life'.

As I sat every night crying as I read and followed the inspiration held within these pages I knew I was on to something. Soon I began meditating every night too. Miracle of miracles, within 3 weeks I was a different person.

Feeling better, I never ended up needing that anxiety medication and I never ended up talking to the psychiatrist at all. This was my breakdown and turning point that shifted everything in my life. My entire path in life was changed from this moment forward. I went to my job, with the same terrifying attorney in charge and the same overburdened tasks but I eventually found the courage to speak up to state my needs and started making different choices.

I bought and obsessively read countless books, immersed myself into live training and coaching and eventually I found me. I found a life I authentically love - even with the bumps and roller coaster rides that are a natural part of our experience. I say yes to things that scare me - including making a transition into being a coach, mentor, teacher, and leader for others just as my mentors have for me. It is my mission that everyone loves themselves and others and their life. No Matter What. I know, that from here, we can literally create world peace.

Looking back, what made it such an important part of your life journey?

As I looked back through my journey with my engineering mind, I analyzed and saw the process I'd gone through along the way and knew it could be simplified into a CODE to follow - what I now call 'Living the Love CODE'. I took my anxiety, resistance, and breakdown and shifted it into feeling alive, joyful, and free. I started processing my life differently, choosing my thoughts so that they supported me rather than run me into the ground. I started to own my own value and trust what felt truly right for me.

We all live such busy, overstressed lives so much so that we're walking around disconnected from ourselves, our family and friends, and all the abundance and possibility around us. I saw there was more to life than the treadmill I was on, so I was able to get connected to my authentic truth and began developing a conscious awareness.

I knew that I needed to take ownership of my life and allow myself time and space to continue exploring. I took a full inventory of my disempowering thoughts, feelings, and behaviours and got to see how I had been processing my life in a way that had ended up causing my anxiety and understood where I needed to take ownership to shift that. I could see how my unstoppable drive and determination to become successful and how I had strived for everything from my childhood got me into this burnt out situation.

I paid attention to how I had been letting my thoughts affect my feelings, behaviours and perception which affected my overall experience, and I chose to decide differently about how I think and process my life instead. As I grew and took on these steps I am now in the flow, I feel alive, I am full of joy as love surrounds me. I have a whole new experience of life! I was in a place that most people dream of being, i.e. a successful lawyer making good money, having good friends, driving a nice car, living in a fancy condo with a nice view, and yet I am in the process of completely changing my life. It is so important to me that you and everyone in the world can say yes to 'turning on the lights' too and that you can shift and transform even more quickly than I did.

Based on the wealth of knowledge, wisdom and experience that you have now what would you have liked to say to yourself back then?

Dear Sweetheart,

I know how much pain you went through as a child beginning when your parents got divorced. I know how deeply painful it was growing up in an environment where you felt unloved and like you had to take care of yourself. You are so loved, cherished and adored, and responsibility is not yours to take on right now. Enjoy being a child, play often, and as you get older you can take on more responsibility as it becomes necessary. Your childhood is meant for having fun and being a kid. When you see something, and you can feel within your whole body that you are connected and that it is right and a definite yes, then say yes before your logical mind can talk you out of it.

Follow your heart and your true desires for living a life you love and being happy. This matters more than achievement and success as defined by society. Stay focused and spend your time, money, and energy on what makes you happy and what you truly desire. Put yourself first, identify your needs and desires, and express them. Don't worry about needing to be right and pleasing others or doing what others want you to do. Other people will project their expectations, opinions, thoughts and feelings onto you but stay true to what you know to be right for you.

You can become successful without working so hard intellectually, grinding through the day, and trying to force things to happen. Rather, you can create and become successful by first connecting with yourself, allowing what is happening, showing up and taking inspired action. Take inspired action instead of actions you think you need to take or actions others want you to take and your life will begin to change for the better. If you are seeking a deeply connected, loving, close, intimate, passionate partnership with an ideal partner (e.g. a romantic partnership) and are struggling to find and meet this person, get help. For example, find a love coach, a love course, a love book, and learn, study, eat, breathe, and sleep love and relationships. Love and relationships require as much energy and focus to create, as anything else in your life you are desiring to create. And yet, we tend to think love and relationships just 'happen'. If you are in a relationship already with someone you feel deeply connected to and who you deeply love but are having issues with, before you decide whether to break up or stay together, get help (e.g. a coach, course, book, or whatever you are called to).

Your worthiness, value and lovability come from much more than your resumé (e.g. being an engineer, attorney, and involved in every activity you can think of). Focus and pay attention to the loving and compassionate part of yourself as much as the determined and driven part of yourself. Take as many vacations as you feel you need to decompress. Travel and explore often. Give yourself time and space to connect with yourself to tune into your inner world, your body, and your soul. Some ways to practice connecting with yourself include meditation, exploring and connecting

" Put yourself first, identify your needs and desires, and express them.
Don't worry about needing to be right and pleasing others or doing what others want you to do. Other people will project their expectations, opinions, thoughts and feelings onto you but stay true to what you know to be right for you. "

-Danielle Morrow-

When you catch a disempowering thought, try to think in that moment of something you are grateful for or remind yourself of the vision of who you choose to be. You consciously unhook from drama and hook onto your vision instead. By taking on these steps, you notice how your experience of life now feels freeing, joyful, and you feel more alive. You feel in flow with what feels good to you and what your body is telling you to say yes to. You express your life the way you want. Experience the life you are meant to live and have in the highest way.

So much love and light, your elder self.

What golden nuggets did you learn from this experience?

Take time to connect with your divine self/soul every single day.

Pay attention to and discover what truly makes you happy instead of solely focusing on achievement.

See obstacles as opportunities to grow and as stepping stones instead of resisting what shows up in your life.

Trust your inner knowing and look within for answers before looking to others.

What would you tell other women who might be experiencing this in their lives?

For all the women who feel stuck, anxious, in breakdown, or like you know there is something more to life than your current experience, I would say take some time to really connect with yourself. This could be through meditation, silence, being in nature, or whatever works for you. Give yourself the space and time to discover what you really desire.

Where in your life is there discontent and what are you longing for in life. Take ownership of who you really want to be and what you're really here to do. You tune into your inner world, integrated through your body and practice listening to your intuition and what feels right for you. You take a full inventory of your disempowering thoughts, feelings, and behaviours, taking ownership of how you've been showing up so that now, releasing any judgment about it, you shift yourself into a more empowering experience of life. You decide differently as you're now paying attention to how your thoughts are affecting your feelings, behaviour, perception and experience. You proactively catch your disempowering thoughts and choices and intentionally choose to shift them to empowering ones.

What are some of the things you would have changed about that situation if you could have?

I wouldn't change anything about this experience because my path has been perfect for me to become who I am today, and I've needed these experiences to grow, evolve and expand my soul.

Any final words?

"The size of your dreams must always exceed your current capacity to achieve them. If your dreams do not scare you, they are not big enough." – Ellen Johnson Sirleaf

How can people get in touch with you and see the work you do?

www.livethelovecode.com
email: danielle@livethelovecode.com

Phoenix Rising –
Move Beyond Emotional Abuse
with Dignity and Grace

Debbie Moore - The High Achievers Coach, and Founder of The Embody Approach to Transformation.

What are you passionate about and how you are contributing to the world?

I am building a Centre of Excellence for High Achievers who are already successful yet stuck in some way. They want powerful development and transformation so that they can break through the barriers and limiting false beliefs that are holding them back. They will then be able to access choice, freedom and resilience and achieve even greater success in relationships, work, life, and contribution.

My passion through this work is to help heal our world, one person, one heart at a time.

Describe a pivotal time in your life that you would like to share:

It was early 2013 and the preceding years had been tough. I was feeling tender having been made redundant in 2012 as well as having lost both my Dad and Mum respectively in 2010 to Alzheimer's and cancer. Those heart-breaking losses came on the back of a divorce in 2007 with a charming man who it turned out, was emotionally abusive, yet that's another story.

For over five and half years I'd been in a relationship with Tom* (*name changed), a man I loved and adored. We'd spoken earlier that morning and he'd mentioned he was off to work, it seemed like a relatively normal day.

I'd been feeling a heavy burden with our relationship particularly of late. There seemed to be very little time for us due, or so it seemed, to his very heavy workload and responsibilities, and I'd put much of my focus and attention on being supportive and caring. After all, we'd gone through so much, we loved one-another, agreed our relationship was exclusive, that we'd be faithful.

We'd discussed growing old together, and when we were together we had great fun and got on well.

So, I reasoned, this burden and heaviness I was feeling deep inside would surely pass.

Later that day, I was in a large warehouse department store shopping with my sister. We were having fun at that point, browsing around independently when suddenly I saw my sister walking towards me, ashen faced. In an instance I felt a life force drain from my body, heart pounding, I knew something was terribly wrong. She approached me and said, "I think Tom is in here with another woman."

My body froze, rooted to the spot, I couldn't move or speak, I felt sick as a shock wave charged through me, like I'd been hit by a truck. Suddenly he appeared at the bottom of the aisle. Taken aback on seeing us, it looked as if for a moment he'd lost his balance. Still frozen and standing there rooted to the spot, I knew something was very, very wrong. It was as if alarm bells were ringing all over my body, my heart was pounding it felt like it was going to explode, yet I couldn't speak, and a dark foreboding dread came over me. He approached me, briefly spoke, kissed me, said he'd call me later, and then hurried away, with the woman with the puzzled expression following behind him.

Everything felt surreal and in slow motion. I shook my head, what was happening? "Somebody help" screamed a voice inside me, I felt like I was watching a movie and in a coma, no-one could hear me, I felt paralyzed. Then, something rose up inside me, an inner strength, shaking and feeling very hot yet with absolute clarity and determination, I slowly moved, walked some 50 feet to the checkouts, and approached Tom, who by that time was near to leaving the store, and drawing on a deeper strength I asked him plainly and clearly "What is going on?" He told me that the woman he was with was his secretary and yet that didn't feel right. She approached us, and I introduced myself by name as his girlfriend. Then, the woman introduced herself, also as his girlfriend. What was going on?

Feeling terrified, yet needing to know, in the moments that followed the truth was revealed. Shockingly it transpired that throughout my years with Tom, the man I thought I was in an exclusive relationship with, had been leading a double life – with both of us, and neither of us knew.

Very briefly we conversed and with profound insight both women involved recognised and agreed that "Tom's lies were so plausible."

With the shock recoiling through my body, my mind suddenly emptied and a voice from deep inside me said, "Leave now, you know enough, anything further will just hurt even more". Somehow, I found the strength and courage to move and say with dignity and grace, "There's no point in me being here." I walked away feeling devastated, angry, bewildered, frightened, sad, and deeply, deeply shocked.

I had no frame of reference for anyone lying like this anywhere in my life before, it didn't make sense, how could anyone do this and be so hurtful? Ricocheting between the emotions generated by his deceit, a recurring question I asked myself again and again was, "Why do I seem to attract men who are ultimately unavailable? What is happening that makes me feel I put myself in similar and increasingly more devastating situations yet with different men?"

I felt blindsided, and I didn't understand it, yet deep inside and without condoning the insidious lies that I'd been told over many years, I turned towards myself, and felt I had to have a part to play in the situation. Was I not good enough? Did I not deserve deep, honest love?

All around me in every other area I had success – wonderful family and friends who I knew loved me, a beautiful and welcoming home, a rewarding and successful career.

Put together, none of this made sense. I felt frightened and alone. How could I ever face anyone again? I felt shame and embarrassment and was heartbroken, devastated, and angry all at the same time. My self-worth in tatters, the magnitude of the shock so great my body jumped at every slight sound, devastated, I felt I was going to die.

Looking back what made it such an important part of your life journey?

Two days later I went to join two associates. We were all training as Somatic coaches. Somatics works with the body as well as the intellect. I literally had to drag myself to meet with them. I desperately wanted to stay in bed, my devastation overwhelming. Yet I was so passionate about somatics, which I'd discovered 10 years earlier. I had immersed myself in the learning, and it was already helping me deeply in life and work.

As soon as I walked through the door my wonderful associates could see before I even said a word that something was terribly wrong, and through the tears I told them what I'd discovered. They could see the trauma I was holding in my body, and my utter distress. Immersed in the learning of how the way we stand and speak affects the way we live and experience life, they gently and compassionately began to feed back to me what they observed and invited me into an exercise. Noticing that when I talked about the 'moment' when I discovered the truth and focused my attention onto it, I looked down, and my body was hunched and constricted. My words, emotions and focus of attention were then on Tom and what had happened.

They compassionately invited me to stand and look forward, eyes on the horizon, to breathe, and let go of any constriction in my body, breathe and gently walk forward. From there I was invited into an intention.

Suddenly and profoundly I felt a shift in my body. It was as if I had a choice.... I said aloud, "I'm committed to my health and wellbeing and moving forward in the world." I kept repeating those words, walking slowly round the room. I noticed the difference between looking down towards the floor and blaming and feeling angry and how that felt so constricting, and standing tall, gently breathing, expanding my body, and purposefully moving and looking forward. In that moment, I felt I had been given the gift of choice – I couldn't change what had happened – I could choose how I responded to it!

I discovered initially through my body, that I could learn from what had happened, so this never, ever, ever happened again. I could make a stand for my healing and wellbeing and ultimately help others.

That was, and is, my choice. In this moment I took personal responsibility, and even in the devastation, embarked on a long healing journey where my first attention was on my well-being.

Based on the wealth of knowledge, wisdom, and experience that you have now what would you have liked to say to yourself back then?

Dear Deb,
JK Rowling once wrote
"Rock bottom became the solid foundation on which I rebuilt my life."

Hold on to that thought and her success as you try to piece the jigsaw together and make sense of what happened. Please, be gentle with yourself as your heart, mind, body, and soul feel shattered and smashed to pieces.

You may jump at every sound as your body ricochets from the trauma you've experienced, and you oscillate between tears, anger and the deepest most profound heart wrenching sadness. Confused and lonely – the very person who you want to reach out to isn't there anymore, you feel betrayed and depressed and a cocktail of so many emotions running constantly.

You'll wonder where your life is heading, yet know this, my darling, hold on and please believe me when I say that this will pass and you will reach a point where your life will develop beyond recognition and surpass your wildest dreams.

Even though you've been through so much, you can't stay home or hide and become invisible and do nothing, you are so much better than that. Deeper inside, through the excruciating pain and feeling that you want to die, you can find a wiser knowing that your life is worth more than this.

I recognise that you'll spend much of that time trying to understand what happened and why you were blindsided. In these moments, and although it may seem counter intuitive, be tenderly open, be vulnerable and discerning, and seek advice and support from your closest family, friends, and professionals in whom you feel you can trust. This will be very challenging at first. You thought you could trust Tom only to have been betrayed yet it's such an important part of your healing. Take what you

===

" You'll start by first learning to trust yourself." The power, freedom and possibilities in our lives start with us and the choices that we make. These words of wisdom stay with me, and I invite you into this space too. "

-Debbie Moore-

===

need and what resonates and let go of anything that doesn't. Really start to learn to trust your inner knowing.

Life won't be perfect, yet you'll learn how to show up and take risks and opportunities in a perfectly imperfect way. At the times when you feel wobbly inside. Turn towards those feelings, acknowledge them, and breathe.

With a trusted coach at your side, you'll be able to take a compassionate look at your 'blind side' and discover that the struggles in your romantic relationships reflected old limiting false beliefs.

Without blame or shame, you'll learn to take personal responsibility and discover the deeper truth of these old limiting false beliefs is part of the key to rebuilding your life.

You'll discover the ways in which you 'self-abandoned ', and deep down inside, you'll see that you'd been holding on to the limiting false belief that you weren't good enough, that others were more important and that you had to be there for them first. Once you see your beliefs clearly, you'll learn to break through them and access the deeper truth of who you really are and that YOU MATTER.

Tenderly, and with self-compassion — yes, it's a very deep insight, my darling — you can feel and have compassion for yourself, as you do for others and, yes, this will be a huge revelation to you. With tenderness, I encourage you to play and notice, just like a child might, and pay attention to your limiting false beliefs and the way you hold your body. Notice how you are standing and sitting, slumped, or expanded, head down or lifted. This will start to give you your power back and although it may not feel like it now, your life will be different.

I encourage you to look inside yourself and ask that deeper, wiser part of you, "What is it that you need?" and look within to discover your true self-worth. It may be rest, meditation, a supportive friend or professional help, a walk, exercise, or something else. Take time, my darling, to listen to yourself, and what you need to heal your shattered self, as you would a child or a beloved friend or family member. Then, step by step, one day at time, act from there for your own well-being.

You'll realise how you hadn't fully understood or embraced self-care, self-love, or self-compassion. As the airlines say, "Put your own oxygen mask on first." In learning to listen and looking after yourself first, and asking for what you need that supports your well-being, you will become so much wiser, and you will heal and grow stronger than before.

As you do this, gently reconnect to being of service and practise being in the act of contribution. Make random acts of kindness – a kind word to a stranger, use a person's name and acknowledge them, suggest a resource that might help a friend, or put on a smile. It's amazing how these small acts can generate joy and a smile in you and others, and in small ways begin to help restore your faith in the goodness of life

Intrigued, you'll discover increasingly about self-compassion, about trusting yourself, and the power of how you hold your body and your limiting old false beliefs. You'll begin to find ways to relax the tension in parts of your body and rediscover how breathing helps the confining tension fade.

From honouring yourself in this way you'll develop the courage to discover more about how the way we show up in relationships and in life and work make a difference. You'll learn how connecting with our bodies and our own inner relationship with ourselves affects the way we live.

You'll train and get certified in so many different areas including Leadership Embodiment Somatic Coaching – which works with the body as well as intellect, Conscious Uncoupling Coaching – which helps people find relief from breakup pain, reclaim personal power, and create a life 'happily ever after' and Feminine Power Coaching - to catalyse and truly awaken women into higher possibilities.

You will be astonished as you discover that you're not the only person in the world who feels the way that you do, or who has experienced something similar in their own life. As you share your stories of betrayal and being lied to, you do so from a place of healing and empowerment to you and to others. You'll be amazed how this resonates with others, and can help support them on their journey of healing and recovery from their trauma and limiting false beliefs.

You'll achieve your ambitious dream of becoming a Somatic Coach and a HR Director. Through life and work, increasingly you find that it may not be easy to stand up and speak out for what's important to you, but you will be amazed how empowering and important it can be.

And then, years later, you'll take a bold step with gratitude, you'll gracefully summon all your courage and "uncouple" from the security of a 30-year career in Human Resources (HR) to focus your energy on your passion for coaching and developing high achievers in innovative transformative ways. This is because you believe so strongly that you are now meant to contribute to life in a different way. You are passionate that the work you do in transforming leaders will, in turn, have a ripple effect of positive change on the planet. Remember that, you too, will achieve so much against great odds. It is the belief and trust in yourself that truly matters. Hold onto it.

You'll discover that over the years you've wanted to help others so much that unknowingly at times you've put others before you and tried to rescue them. You'll learn it's not your job to rescue others, it is for them to do. They too have their lessons to learn. You can hold a safe space and offer love, support, and encouragement, recognising that their healing is their journey. Being there for people in a healthy adult way is of value.

As you look back when you reach 55 years of age, you'll see that this "dark night of the soul" was a huge stepping stone, and one where you chose to be a Phoenix and rise from the ashes. A time where you chose to heal, learn, be graceful, dignified, and to move forward. A time when you chose to help yourself and be of service to help others break through what is blocking them. Yes, there will still be days when you'll feel lonely, exhausted and sad, and that's ok. Remember to be gentle with yourself as this too will pass. You'll continue in your practice to be skilled and visible, no more hiding under a bushel.

You'll learn that you are enough the way that you are. That also means you choose to learn where your 'edge' is, your lack of skill, inexperience, or capacity, and to develop those edges. Learn to feel your feelings, and

71

don't ruminate on how others have hurt you. Once you've felt them, let them pass.

Keep listening to the wisdom of your body, and exercise and eat well. You'll discover that rest and creativity are such an important part of a living life in balance. Be amazed at how much you come to love furniture painting, yoga, and for a time, kickboxing too!

You'll discover the power of forgiveness and that this takes time and attention over months, if not years. You'll learn to understand that forgiveness is a choice to let go of resentment and thoughts of revenge, and perhaps even reach a place of understanding, empathy, and compassion. It's not reconciling, nor is it forgetting, justifying, or excusing what the other person did. Rather, it helps achieve a sense of peace. By letting go you give up your role as the victim. Stop ruminating and embrace moving on in a wiser way. As Mahatma Gandhi said, "The weak can never forgive. Forgiveness is the attribute of the strong."

Finally, my darling, embrace an attitude of gratitude, and know that this leads to more happiness and well-being. Your rock bottom became the solid foundation on which you rebuilt your life, and know and appreciate all that you have learnt, contributed, and experienced, and have hope that the best is yet to come.

With love, gratitude, and grace,

Deb

What golden nuggets did you learn from this experience?

When I sat devastated in my coach's office I asked her, "How can I ever trust a man again?" Her words stay with me. Compassionately she replied, "You'll start by first learning to trust yourself." The power, freedom and possibilities in our lives start with us and the choices that we make. These words of wisdom stay with me, and I invite you into this space too.

I prioritised my healing and wellbeing first, and went on a journey of self-discovery that lasted many months, and continues.

I discovered the power of deciding to go 'no contact' with my former partner, how trauma is held in the body and how important it is to release that as well as the power of self-compassion.

As my experience, knowledge and understanding has expanded so did my selection process of what I allowed to enter my sacred space....my mind.

Guard your mind against those things that limit your possibilities and open it to those which will expand your opportunities.

Life is too short to hold grudges. Peoples' perceptions of any given situation are always different based on our experience, knowledge and interactions, so forgive and release and let go of what doesn't serve you.

What would you tell other women who might be experiencing this in their lives?

You're not going mad, neither are you alone. Sadly, there are people out there who are emotionally abusive and are so damaged and hurt in their own lives that they hurt others. Know that 'hurt people, hurt people'.

The person you want to turn to is no longer there having betrayed you. You may feel tempted to go back, and it's at this very point you have a choice and that is to focus your attention on you, your health and wellbeing - physically, emotionally, and spiritually.

You can break free from the patterns of the past and your hurt. Your future can be brighter, happier, and healthier. Reach out for support and share what's been happening with people you trust. Start with the very basics, learn to be compassionate with yourself. Heartbreak is real, so pay attention to the basics: sleep, rest, gentle exercise, and nutrition, and keep yourself safe. Gently take one step at a time towards your healing and wholeness. You can do it and you don't need to do it alone. Ask for help and support.

Learn and listen out for what are known as 'red flags' in relationships - indicators that something needs to be questioned or otherwise validated. Often these are clues that something may be trouble in the future. This could be a hunch, a good intuitive sense to help you process what you're really feeling. Learn to have the courage to trust what you feel. That hunch is probably right!

What are some of the things you would have changed about that situation if you could have?

I wish I had known and appreciated that I was running a false limiting belief system that others were more important than me. I wish that I'd trusted my inner knowing and focused my attention more on how I felt when I was with Tom, and more importantly, how I felt when I wasn't with him. There were so many red flags, yet I trusted him more than my inner hunches and intuition. I did speak up at times when things felt 'off' in the relationship. What I didn't do was piece all those together earlier.

I had an inner guidance in both my body and my beliefs that something was off, yet back then I didn't have the skills to really listen to that and put myself and my wellbeing first.

This pattern, I now know, had been building in my being and unconscious for years and becoming my rock bottom, and subsequently, the biggest turning point in my life.

This experience like so many others has shaped who I am, and yes, there are times that I wish I had learnt to trust myself first in my relationships, particularly with men. As I look back, I'm proud that I took a stand for me and that I learned to turn this around.

I also look back with a strange mix of sadness and compassion for men in my life, and what may have been going on in their lives, their self-esteem, and their minds to think that controlling behaviour, living a double life or emotional abuse was acceptable. And I also recognise that there are very many good honest men out there doing their best too, and I recognise that I had a part to play. I took personal responsibility for self-abandoning and the part that played in my relationships once I realised what was really happening through me.

Any final words?

Before I met Tom, and in previous relationships as well, I thought women who experienced emotional abuse were nothing like me – I'm successful, intelligent, and fundamentally happy. Yet, over the past few years, I've heard this time and time again; emotional abuse is happening everywhere to women just like me – bright, successful, high achievers. That's what's driven me to speak out now. You're not alone and you can change this – I did and so can you.

It is my hope now that for people finding themselves stuck and in pain from past or present relationship breakup, or in life or work, they chose possibility. By finding support or someone to work with in a safe space you too can work through barriers or limiting false beliefs and transform the sorrow or 'stuckness' into strength and new-found personal power and your best life yet.

Trust yourself. You do have choices in your life – take one step at a time, you can realise all your potential and authenticity – and always know that YOU MATTER!

How can people get in touch with you and see the work you do?

Email: debbie@debbiemoorecoaching.com
www.debbiemoorecoaching.com
Phone: (+44) 07808783483

Your Health is Your Greatest Wealth – Don't Lose It Chasing Success

Izabella Niewiadomska - The Energy Entrepreneur: Performance Coach, Health Strategist, Speaker, Author, Founder and Director of the Contribution Conference and Total Wellness.

What are you passionate about and how you are contributing to the world?

My passion is to work with people globally and make a difference in their lives. Helping people with their health, performance and quality of life, stems from my personal experience of losing my own health to stress when I was just 23.

Since that happened I've been on a quest, dedicating my life to learning from the best and practising anything I could to regain my physical, mental and emotional health. My mission is to empower people to transform their lives with simple, practical and effective strategies to achieve long-term health and sustainable success in life!

Your Health is your Ultimate Wealth!

Describe a pivotal time in your life you would like to share:

Have you ever been in a situation where everything was going well in your life, according to plan, and then suddenly something happened...Boom! Your life turned upside down, shattering your confidence and in the process, you discovered that life will never be the same again?

Maybe you have found yourself pushing way too hard, trying to meet your own high expectations of what life and work should be like and have paid a high price for it?

Maybe you've found yourself trapped in a place, circumstance or simply in your head absorbed with your own thoughts, not able to see a way out, feeling lost and helpless, with no control over yourself or the situation?

Perhaps it was your pride, your strong sense of being independent that prevented you from asking for help when you needed it the most. Or maybe you didn't allow yourself to express your emotions when the time was right, that cost you your health, relationship, happiness or even success?

Well, that was me 31 years ago. If you were there with me on a sunny September day, you would have seen me lying on a hospital bed in a room that was oozing with white coldness, a total contrast to the warmth outside my window. Three men were standing in front of my bed, a doctor, a translator and the leader of my country's cultural delegation. The doctor spoke, looking me straight in the eyes. I didn't understand his words, he was German. The translator explained... I had been diagnosed with a panic attack, a very severe case. I was told that my body had been brought to a state of a total exhaustion and my organs were starting to shut down.

After they left the room many thoughts flashed through my mind. I nearly died, or so I thought. I kept asking myself, "How did I get here?"

Just last night I was having fun with my friends at the cultural festival in Germany and today I am in the hospital. What happened?

I tried to remember the events of the last night. The evening weather was surprisingly warm for a mid-September night. Although the event was in a lovely outdoor area, you couldn't feel any breeze. The air was hot and humid, so that you could feel every piece of clothing sticking to your sweaty skin and body.

The festival was in a full swing with hundreds of people walking through the narrow alleys between large tents, where there was music, dancers and food. People were queueing for their turn to buy something to eat and drink, as I was too. As I waited I chatted with my friends about everything and nothing.

All of a sudden, I started to feel uneasy. My neck got very hot and I was slightly weak in my knees. The need for fresh air suddenly became the only thing I was able to focus on. I looked around and saw a sea of people around me, standing so close to each other that I couldn't see a way out. Instantly I felt trapped!

As I noticed a tingling sensation in my hands I turned to my friends to ask for help, to tell them that something strange was happening to me, but I couldn't say a word. Almost like in a dream when you want to scream and you can't. My tongue felt hard, like a piece of wood. I couldn't move. I couldn't speak. And the next thing I remembered I was waking up in the hospital.

I asked myself again, "How did I get here?" I looked back at my life, a life beyond the events of the night before and thought, "Was it all worth it?"

Was it worth it to work so hard, just to prove that I could do everything without any help, too proud to ask for it anyway, building my career to a point that I ended up in the hospital with a case of severe panic attacks, nearly losing my life?

How could I not realise that stress, long working hours and hectic lifestyle might lead to a burnout, especially when combined with some bad habits I had accrued along the way? I kept smoking heavily, sometimes up to 40 cigarettes a day to keep me going and drinking far too much socially.

I thought I will be ok. After all I was young, strong and healthy and I felt invincible but this time I had pushed my body way too far.

Looking back what made it such an important part of your life's journey?

I believe everything happens for a reason. Every experience serves and prepares you for your journey in life. Somehow, I always knew that.

However, my experience shattered my confidence because for the first time in my life I wasn't in control. I didn't know how to deal with it, what to do, how to regain my health, how to take back control over my body and life. My world, where pretty much everything had come to me easily, had collapsed and I just wasn't expecting it.

Every time I had a panic attack I had to be taken back to the hospital as my whole body was overtaken by a full body paralysis, loss of speech and a terrible fear of death. I hated the fact I had no control over my body or my fearful thoughts. I was young but felt old and tired.

Losing my health and getting panic attacks put a different perspective on everything. The experience humbled me and helped me to develop humility, resilience and a mental strength I never knew I had. It also triggered my interest in health and wellbeing.

During my recovery I was prepared to do whatever it took to regain my health. I immersed myself in the study of herbs, nutrition, natural remedies, yoga and meditation. Later I became completely bewitched by the power of the mind, modern neuroscience, the energy of the universe, the power of mindset and focus, healing ways of thinking and even quantum physics. What I learned to help myself, I was able to use later to help others.

At 27 I found myself at the crossroads in life. I realised that journalism, was not for me anymore. I knew my passion was to work with people and make a difference in their lives, I just didn't know how.

All I knew was I wanted to be healthy, happy and fulfilled, to develop strategies that would prevent me from another bout of burnout and anxiety and I wanted the same for other people, so they too would not end up like me – trapped and lost on a hospital bed.

I followed my gut instinct and the solutions started to present themselves to me one by one in the form of different opportunities.

Based on the wealth of knowledge, wisdom and experience that you have now what would you have liked to say to yourself back then?

Dearest Izabella,
I know you are fearful at the moment. You have just woken up and saw that your mummy and daddy are not here, their bed next to yours is empty.

What happened? Where are they? Have they abandoned me? Don't they love me anymore? Why is it dark? Why am I locked in and why can't I leave this room?

Izabella, I know there must be a lot of questions flying through your little bright head right now. Hush now, please sit down close to me, and let me explain to you what has happened.

" Health is your ultimate wealth - Without it you have nothing "

-Izabella
Niewiadomska-

Relax, you are not by yourself and you never will be. I'm here with you. Your mummy and daddy haven't abandoned you. They never would, you are their life, their only child, and they absolutely love you, you know that, don't you? You've always been spoiled with their love from the moment you opened your eyes to greet this world.

Your mummy and daddy are in the building next door, dancing and will be back shortly. They saw you were asleep and so they decided to pop out for an hour, they didn't expect you to wake up before they got back.

I know it can be a bit scary to wake up in a dark room, not knowing what's happening with your parents, to find them gone, and to realise you are by yourself, but you are a brave girl.

And although you might feel trapped, being locked in a room that you can't leave, you should know, the only reason your parents locked the door was to keep you safe, so no one would enter the room while they were not here. So, you see you are not trapped. You are just specially protected.

I love that you were so courageous and resourceful to get on that chair, switch the lights on and start banging on the door so someone would hear your voice screaming for help. It worked! A stranger passing by heard you and has already notified your parents. They are on their way and will be back here in a few minutes and will comfort you with their hugs, words and kisses.

Know as we sit quietly and wait for their return that later in life you will learn that things are not always as they seem. You will understand that you have the power to decide and choose the meaning you attach to every experience. However, these emotions of being abandoned at this very moment will have a huge impact on your life. This experience will affect you emotionally and create a behavioural pattern that will play an important role throughout your life.

It will lay the foundations for some of your emotional patterns and fears. Emotions that will reappear like ghosts from the past to haunt you, especially at times when you will feel most vulnerable. Sometimes even a simple misunderstanding in communication with those you love will be interpreted as lack of appreciation and acceptance, and you will feel abandoned yet again, not loved. Fortunately, you will learn how to quickly bounce back from your low points stronger than before, you will learn more about the psychology of human needs and build your emotional muscles and intelligence.

So, as we are waiting for your mummy and daddy to return, let me tuck you into your bed and I will tell you a few great things about your future life.

Let me share some of the important details that might help you on your journey through life. You are so independent that you might be thinking right now I don't need this and that what I'm about to tell you will go straight over your head but I'm going to tell you anyway, so you might as well just listen. See for yourself if any of this makes sense. Take what you find useful and discard the rest, it is your choice. You are in control, you are in charge of your life and you always will be, and that is another one of the leading patterns in your life.

Izabella, you are born with the natural qualities of a high performer, with huge potential to achieve great things, to have your dreams come true and to truly make a difference in people's lives. I have travelled far into the future and had a good look at your life. Went nearly as far as your 55th birthday. That must seem incredibly old to you right now.

I can tell you though, at 55 you will look at least 10 years younger. Daily Mail newspaper will call you a "super-ager". You will be fitter than many women younger than you and will be very proud to have the metabolic age of a teenager. You will want to inspire others to achieve same results.

Both men and women, will want you to coach them and attend your workshops. Companies will invite you to speak for their organisations. They will see your passion for health and contribution and will want to learn your health strategies, energy and performance habits so that they can use them to improve and live extraordinary lives too.

At the age of 50 you will challenge yourself to start running and will go from a complete novice, to completing a 100-kilometre ultra- run three years later, to raise money for a limbless veteran's charity. This experience will lead to your strategies how to perform better and recover quicker and achieve goals.

Believe or not when you turn 50, major national newspapers and magazines will want to interview you to discover more about your achievements and the secrets to your youthful, delicious looks and inexhaustible energy.

You will have an incredible life, Izabella. As the only child, you will be spoiled with love, cherished and admired by your parents and family. I know that even at this young age you realise how blessed you are.

The incredible love of your parents for you, will comfort you, give you strength and will teach you how to share, give and express love. You will be greatly influenced by their values and qualities and many of them become your own. They will encourage you to speak your mind although sometimes you will embarrass them in public with your blunt remarks, still they let you just be yourself. Thanks to this you will grow up to be bold, confident and fearlessly independent.

Always smiling and full of happy energy, you will be a natural charmer. Your fascination with people and things will be inexhaustible. They will describe you as 'quicksilver' as you can hardly stay still, eager to explore the world and ask hundreds of questions.

You know you were born with an incredible intuition that will guide you through life, but you need to learn to trust your gut feelings more because when you do, you will make better decisions. When you don't, when you let your doubts and fears dictate your decisions, you will suffer and miss out on the beautiful things and experiences in life. So, please start to trust yourself.

Somehow, you will instinctively understand that everything happens for a reason. You will have your own logic, and despite your quick, analytical brain you will always find a philosophical explanation as to why things sometimes didn't go as you planned or wanted. Your favourite phrase at those times will be: "It was just not meant to be".

This quality will really serve you well, because when faced with many adversities and challenges, instead of being frustrated, disappointed and depressed, like other people in such situations, you will be fine, never losing your enthusiasm and zest for life. Every time life will try to knock you down, you will quickly pick yourself up again. Just like that.

You will also develop an incredible ability to quickly adjust to change and new circumstances. This ability will be very useful, when at 27 you will decide to move to the UK where you will start a new life from a scratch. Perceived initially by some people as "nobody" you will overcome challenges, will rebuild and create a successful life in a new country, gaining respect and admiration as you go.

Your dad will be your hero; however, it will be your uncle you will want to impress. He will often challenge you at family gatherings saying, "Izabella can't do this," or "Izabella will not be able to do that..." which will make you determined to prove yourself to him, to show him that you can, often biting your bottom lip, holding back tears, emotions and frustration to achieve something you were not keen to do.

He will laugh with admiration and pride at your determination. This experience will be very valuable and will have both a positive and slightly negative impact on you and your habitual patterns in life. It will teach you to be cautious when expressing your emotions, and it will also teach you that you can do anything when you put your mind to it.

As you start working, this determination will see you solve many things, you will be known as the person to go to when something needs to be resolved.

Work will bring you joy but it will also put you out of balance. You will enjoy meeting fascinating people and start to take on more and more new responsibilities. They will bring variety and fresh excitement into your life. Unfortunately, you will end up trying to do too many things at the same time. This will bring a new level of stress because you will push yourself to the limits to prove yourself in a male-dominated environment, like you did for your uncle.

You will hate to say NO to people and will always agree to help them, fearing that by letting them down you might be abandoned, not accepted and left as an outsider, not loved and it will all stem from your experience and the emotions you are experiencing right now, when you woke up alone in this room and felt abandoned by your parents.

Although you will understand that it is wise to ask for help from experts and professionals, you struggle with asking for help for yourself, for something you need to do. Somehow on your journey you will view asking for help as a lack of your ability, as a weakness.

Interestingly, people will be always keen to help you, but refusing their help, especially the help offered by those who love you will make your intimate relationships difficult. You will not make it easy for people to love you, because they will often feel rejected and not needed by your actions. If they do love you deeply enough to agree to your independent ways, you will perceive them as weak and will not fully appreciate them, withdrawing from the relationship.

Although your life will turn out wonderfully, I do need to warn you about a time that will come when that control that you hold onto so tightly will be ripped away from you. At 23 you will suddenly learn what it feels like to lose the main source of your confidence and the certainty that you can always figure things out by yourself.

Izabella, you have grown up in a world where you grew too strong to be able to connect with your soul, too proud to allow yourself to show your vulnerability and ask for help when you needed it most. This world will lead to your body being over-stressed and over-worked to the point of total exhaustion and as a result you will develop scary panic attacks.

During this time, you will learn to appreciate the physical and psychological impact that these panic attacks will have on your life, the emotional struggle you will go through to get your health back and the transformation of your thinking to regain your confidence and control.

You will find that the person you once were, who was always in control, fearlessly independent, living the life the way you wanted on your own terms will need for once, to ask for help. At your very worst you will sleep with the lights on and ask your mum to hold your hand because you will be afraid that you might die if you were by yourself in a dark room. You will be afraid to leave the house by yourself, in fear you might suffer a panic attack and help will not arrive in time to rescue you and you will die. These experiences will help you to reconnect with your emotions and your mum.

You will absolutely hate the fact you have no control over your body, fears and emotions. You will feel lost, helpless and betrayed. You have never liked taking medication and now you have to take many. There will be a month that you will feel like a zombie...falling asleep, waking up to eat, taking another dose of medications and sleep again for hours. You will not like these side effects and will start to look for alternatives. Thankfully a family member will introduce you to a herbal pharmacy run by monks.

Now the zombie will be transformed for a while into a little witch in the kitchen, brewing several different herbs three times per day. Friends will laugh at you lovingly, and you will laugh at yourself with them. You will not care. All you will be interested in is getting your health back. You will be prepared to do anything, so you won't have to go back to the hospital again, and yet you will from time to time, usually when you don't get enough sleep or get stressed. Each time you will be convinced you are dying.

Your journey to full recovery won't be easy and will take time. In the process you will discover the power of Intelligent Supplementation, the power of cellular nutrition to feed the body on a cellular level, to ensure your organs function and perform at their best. This will give you the certainty you were searching for that your body is getting everything it needs to protect you and keep you healthy.

Your panic attacks will be a blessing in disguise. They will be a tool you will use to dismantle the person you've been up to that point and start rebuilding and creating the person who can connect to your purpose in life, impacting on people and global health.

As you get back in control, this time you have a new knowing that being vulnerable, asking for help and accepting help is not a weakness, *it is a strength that connects you to other people and enables you to love completely, and live fully. Experiencing variety of deep emotions, discovering your own solutions will be an amazing asset in your work with people, who find you absolutely understand them and their challenges and they will trust you are the person to lead them to their desired results.*

Are you excited now knowing what your life will be like? Dry those tears and wipe away your fear as your parents are at the door. Let me hug you and kiss and bless you for your journey ahead, I look forward to seeing you there.

What golden nuggets did you learn from this experience?

Health is your ultimate wealth.

Do you think about health when you are well? Probably not. Many people rarely do, busy working and juggling daily responsibilities, we tend to take good health for granted. I'm fine, we say, I don't have any problems so why would I need to focus on health? Yet simple tiredness, a slight headache or indigestion can bring us to our knees and then we focus all our energy on getting better.

We promise to look after ourselves and start making changes. However, the minute we are back on our feet, we forget about promises, we don't maintain the changes, and we go back to the usual busy pace of living. Until the next time, when life intervenes and remind us how important our health truly is.

I've learned the hard way, that health is a gift and without it you have nothing!

What would you tell other women who might be experiencing this in their lives?

Don't be too hard on yourself.

Life is not about perfection, as perfection is an illusion. Be happy and satisfied with the smallest progress you make, with every lesson you learn.

Strive to be better, to do better but remember to enjoy the journey, treasure every moment on the way because life is perfect the way it is. Everything is perfect as it is, including you. Love yourself the way you are. Every imperfection you see in the mirror is a part of the perfection that is YOU!

It's ok to ask for help and to accept it.

Don't apologize or feel guilty if you need to ask for help, but at the same time, don't be too proud to accept help when it is offered with genuine intention. Accepting help doesn't mean you can't do it yourself. You can, however, you don't have to.

True joy and happiness come from things that we share, that we do together. So, start sharing the overload of work and the responsibilities, as this will bring balance into your life.

I love the way Jim Rohn explains this, he says: "One person doesn't make a family, one person doesn't make a symphony orchestra, one person doesn't make a community. Each of us need all of us, and all of us need each of us."

So, don't try to prove to the world that you can do everything by yourself at the expense of your health and relationships.

What are some of the things you would have changed about that situation if you could have?

Everything played a part and was important and essential for me to become the person I am today. It prepared me for my role in life now, to truly discover my purpose. I wouldn't really change anything. I would only try to learn my lessons faster and be more focused to implement them.

Any final words?

Live fully, live with passion, never be afraid of making mistakes. Do the best you can, and when you have done your best, be proud of yourself and celebrate.

Master the power of daily Gratitude. Be grateful for every person and every experience. They're your life teachers and mentors. They carry messages and lessons you need to help you reach your full potential. Gratitude has the power to transform your health and your life.

How can people get in touch with you and see the work you do?

I love the human touch and would love to speak with you directly so please feel free to text me on +447968 953149

www.izabellaniewiadomska.com
LinkedIn - www.linkedin.com/in/izabellaniewiadomska/
Twitter: @nutritiousmind
www.facebook.com/izabella.niewiadomska.7

From Striving to Thriving

Sarah Sparks, CEO and Founder of the Choose to Thrive Movement.

What are you passionate about and how you are contributing to the world?

I don't want others to suffer like I did which is why I'm building the world's most supportive community-based resource for stressed people to ignite their spark in a safe and secure environment.

This community is where we can share the most powerful "how to" strategies to help improve all areas of your relationships, wealth, health and wellbeing, so we can reduce levels of stress, anxiety, depression and burnout.

I believe that everyone can be more successful in their relationships, wealth, health and wellbeing when they are supported in the right way, with the right resources and by the right community.

Describe a pivotal time in your life you would like to share:

Come with me back to July 21st, 1995. It's a beautiful, beautiful day. The sun has not long risen and that clear early morning feeling is everywhere. The trees are dappled with that fresh morning sunlight and you can hear the blackbirds singing their early morning song.

Everything is calm and tranquil.

We're sitting in the back of a taxi speeding along Kings Road. There's no traffic. It was that early.

But this calm and peaceful exterior was in sharp contrast to how I felt inside. I felt sick.

The thought of breakfast made me wretch. I been up all night taking phone calls from Asia and had got very little sleep. I was Head of Financial Regulation and was meant to sign off million-dollar trades but this one I just didn't understand. My brain wouldn't work properly; I just couldn't think straight. I was in a panic and needed to speak to my boss, someone who I called Slippery Jim.

We got to the office in record time and I made my way up to my office on the fifth floor at Goldman Sachs. I had one of the best views overlooking the city of London and the Dome of St Paul's. It looked stunning that morning basked in that early morning sunshine, but I had no time to enjoy the view.

My boss, Slippery Jim, was slippery all right, slippery by name and slippery by nature. He was one of those plump New Yorkers with a sweaty handshake and sweaty complexion. A bit of a Danny DeVito but without the personality. You know the type. I spotted him across the hallway. "Jim, Jim, have you got a minute? I need your help."

"What's up Sarah? Why are you interrupting my cawfee? Sooorrrrry, no time today, got back-to-back meeeeetings. I'm sure you can handle it. Give me a call at the end of the day and tell me it's done."

With that, he turned his back and walked away.

"What an arsehole, what a fucking arsehole! How could he do that to me? I hardly ever asked for his help and when I do ……. How could he walk away and not even listen to me? Doesn't he realise what's at stake? We don't have enough regulatory capital to get this wrong."

Fast forward two weeks, and I'm sitting in another office. This one was dark with oak panelled walls and a stern, yet familiar, face opposite me. It was an Asian man with a sharp, pointy nose and thick black hair.

"You know why you're back at the Priory Hospital Sarah, don't you?
You've been completely overdoing it again. Long, long hours, skipping breakfast, living off coffee, lunch on the run, using wine to relax, no breaks, working weekends. It's not surprising you're back. Did you not learn anything from the last stay? This time I'm going to have to keep you in longer and get you back on medication. Sarah, this can't keep happening. This has to stop!"

"I know, I know, I just don't have a choice, I have to work this way. It's expected of me. I wouldn't be able to do my job if I didn't. What would others think?

I'd probably lose my job and then what?
I can't afford to do that. My husband's business isn't doing that well."

"Stop there! Of course, you have a choice. Everyone has a choice.
Does it say in your contract that you have to work these crazy hours? No, it doesn't.
Does it say in your contract you're not entitled to breaks and you have to work weekends? No, it doesn't.
Does it say in your contract that you should work so hard you drive yourself into a mental hospital? No, it doesn't.
Of course, you have a choice, Sarah, you're just not choosing wisely right now."

Oh my god, he was so right. He was right about everything.

That was the pivotal moment for me. That was my wake-up call. I had to start choosing wisely and putting my health and wellbeing on my list of priorities. Not at the bottom but somewhere near the top.

Realising that I was choosing every step of the way was a bolt out of the blue. If I said yes to working late, I was saying no to spending time with my husband, friends and family. If I said yes to working weekends, I was saying no to going to the gym, or spending time doing something I loved. Of course, it wasn't easy, but I woke up to the fact that whether I liked it not I was choosing how my life was. I didn't know how it was going to be possible to choose more wisely and it took a long time to shift things for sure but I got there, well the truth is you very rarely get there, but I'm certainly well on my way now. The reality is I'm a 'work in progress' but now I put my health, particularly my mental health, front of stage these days.

Based on the wealth of knowledge, wisdom and experience that you have now, what would you have liked to say to yourself back then?

My dearest, darling Sarah,
I can't tell you how pleased and excited I am to hear your news. Who'd have thought that this little scrap of a girl who failed her 11 plus would become an Executive Director of Goldman Sachs. I am so, so proud of you. It's so well deserved.

You have worked your nuts off and gone way beyond what most people would have put themselves through to get here and you've done it. You have made it.

It was so lovely to see you celebrate too with your Mum, Dad and siblings all around you. Your Dad was so proud he almost burst with joy when he shared with the gathered party why we had cracked open the champagne. That pride from a parent is unbeatable and something I hope one day you too will enjoy.

I'm sorry to put a dampener on your celebrations but I'm worried about you and I want to share my concerns. Although this is an amazing achievement, I want to also point out that this is a trap. A trap that I see many women like you and I make. We've worked hard, we deserve what we have achieved and yet there is a big sacrifice to make. Little do you know the painful price that you will pay over the next few years and how that will impact your life forever. I know that you feel invincible. I did too. I felt I could achieve anything and that life was on my side. I would work hard and get everything I dreamt of.

The wonderful husband, the beautiful family, the nice house, smart car, the exotic holidays; all of it will be just desserts for the hard work I put in. From the outside, that lifestyle seems amazing doesn't it? And at some level it is. But very few people see the sacrifice that goes with it. The long hours, the missing out on family and friends, the hurried, rushed moments spent with your husband, the smiles you put on to say that everything was FINE*, the exhaustion, the inability to think straight, the fear of being found out, or doing something wrong, the fear of not keeping up or falling behind the pack. It's stressful alright, but the sad thing is that it seems normal. Even the anxiety and sleepless nights become normal. The erratic breathing and the gulping for air that your body is driven to in this stressed state becomes normal.

And then there are the years and years of yearning and wanting to have a baby and becoming the mother you always dreamed of. That doesn't happen. All you see around you is your friends and family procreating with ease and there you are struggling. Not being able to really talk about it

" **Life is short and precious so don't let someone else dictate your life for you. Wake up, take control of the wheel, and enjoy the ride.** "

-Sarah Sparks-

Spring was worse because everywhere you looked nature was procreating as it should be and there were prams everywhere and yet... nothing. No sign of hope, just your regular period that you can tell is coming despite all your hopes. And then somehow, you're signed up for fertility treatment. How inhumane that is, the lack of intimacy, the physical blunt instruments they use to make you produce lots of eggs, the daily injection you have to give yourself into your stomach. How your husband can't cope, looks the other way and leaves you on your own until it's his turn and he pleasures himself as his contribution. How come it's so unfair this distribution of effort and heartache. He won't speak about it and plays it matter of fact and you want to scream and punch your pillow until there are no feathers left.

It hurts, really hurts, and all the time you keep working and pretending nothing is untoward, everything is fine*. You hold back the tears when you see your period has started and come out of the bathroom an hour later having finally composed yourself. The excuses, the lies, the torture. And you keep working and pretending that everything is fine*.

Then that one time when your period didn't come and you were so excited, so overwhelmed, you found it difficult to concentrate at work or sleep at night and then, a few weeks later after hope had kicked in......again...... nothing. The first drops of blood turned the hope into another kick in the stomach.

And so, the years go on and the IVF attempts come and go until they say, "Enough. You're too old. It isn't going to happen. It's not meant to be. You must come to terms with your lot." But how can you do that all of a sudden when you have been hoping month after month, year after year, that this might be the moment when your whole life changes.

And then there are the frozen embryos. What happens to them? The clinic tells you that you have no choice other than to let them perish. And I believed them. How could that possibly be right? Surely it would have been worth putting them inside me just in case. But I was in such a state I believed everything I was told and all the time kept that smile on my face whilst holding down that job as if everything was fine*.

Letting those embryos perish was one of the hardest things I have had to do, and I remember carrying them around in my handbag for days before I could let them go. I knew it was crazy and I needed to do something, so I spent ages thinking about how I wanted to honour them and all the while my husband wasn't interested and didn't want to talk about it. He did agree to come with me to a quiet place on the Thames in London and empty the vial with our dead babies onto the evening tide.

My heart broke and still does every time I walk by. I remember these unborn children of mine every day and wonder what they would have been up to now if they had had their earthly moment. Crazy as it might seem, I have put stone follies in my garden to remember them and I recall the next-door neighbour's child, who can only have been 5 at the time, leaning out of the window and saying, "Why are there dead people in the garden?"

So, I know they are there and their souls are now somewhere else, I suspect doing great work and shining. To me they are like the sparkles you see on crisp fallen snow in the sunshine, or the sparkle in a drop of dew and the sun reflected in the ripples of water. They are the light.

And what can I tell you of marriage? Well I think marriage itself is a great constitution, but it requires effort and hard work. And lots of it. But it can't be one sided. Both of you have to work hard.

I fell in love with a man who was besotted with me. He loved the way I looked, the clothes I wore, the prestigious job I had, the title, the money, the car, the lifestyle. But when those things were no longer me he got disillusioned, disappointed and even angry. So often he used to say to me, "You're not the woman I married" and I would be proud and excited about that and he.....finally walked away.

And you know what? The galling thing was I thought we had an agreement for life. I thought we had both signed up for 'until death do us part', 'in good times and in bad', 'in sickness and in health' but no, he was there only when I looked the part, had the title and when I could make a significant financial contribution. When I no longer wanted that and wasn't capable of it, he was gone. God, that hurt. And there I was thinking that he loved me unconditionally. How wrong I was.

Don't get me wrong, we had what appeared from the outside to be a very successful 18 years of marriage. We didn't argue, we were always loving towards each other and we were the most amazing hosts. People loved our company and our parties. Again, I kept up the smiles and the pretence. And then there were all the trappings. After being told we were not destined to be parents we threw ourselves into 'things'. I remember my husband saying, "He who has most things wins" and that was what it was like. Several houses, ski apartments, classic yachts, cars, even more exotic holidays. You name it, we had it, but it didn't make us happy, well it didn't make me happy anyway. In fact, far from it. I was miserable. Surrounded by beautiful things with every reason to be happy and content, but miserable and as more and more time went by the less and less happy I became.

You see, it wasn't me. I have learnt that it doesn't matter how much stuff you have, it doesn't make you happy. What makes me happy is being with people I really love and who love me warts and all (and let me tell you I have warts, big warts) and to do simple things. Dinner with friends, enjoying the view, walking in the sunshine, walking in the rain.

The more and more I realise as I get older that it's the simple things in life that make me happy. I don't need stuff, I need moments, and the wherewithal to appreciate them. Life is good when you are grateful for the small things.

So, my darling Sarah, beware of what is to come. It is going to difficult. It's going to push you beyond what you thought was possible and you'll break. You'll break and be broken for many years. You'll spend months and months in a psychiatric hospital and years and years under psychiatric care. You'll be angry and bitter and do your best not to show it and pretend everything is fine*, but it's there.

But you know what? This is all meant to be. These difficult and challenging experiences that you have no choice but to live through will be the making of you. It will allow you to discover who you are and what's important. No longer will you be swayed by your family dynamics or your selfish husband, but you will find yourself in all of this and shine.

It will show you where and how you can make a difference in the world and you won't want to change a thing. All the heartache and suffering will be worthwhile.

Trust me I know.

My darling Sarah, now is the time to start believing in your brilliance and trusting that you know what's good and right for you and you don't need others to tell you how to live your life. What you have to bring to the world will shine brightly. You too are the sparkle that is all around.

I love you and I'm always here for you.

Your loving elder self,

Sarah

> ** I found out in the psychiatric hospital that FINE stood for Fucked up, Insecure, Neurotic and Emotional.*

What golden nuggets did you learn from this experience?

Well, as I look back on my whole life, I can see that the start of people pleasing behaviour started when I was newly born. My elder sister who was born with a hole in the heart wasn't expected to live very long so they rushed ahead and had me. But there was lots of worry and anxiety in the house, quite understandably, I soon discovered that my crying for attention didn't work as well as being my smiley happy self. I even remember my mother saying to me early on that no one wants to be with someone who doesn't smile. And there it was. I took that on board and smiled, pretended everything was fine and pleased people from then on. But as you can see the price was high. I lost myself and didn't know who I was or what I wanted. I can see from a large family point of view, and even in my marriage, it was much easier and nicer if I melded in. But that didn't allow me to blossom and shine. If only I had stayed connected with that little person, goodness knows where life would have taken me.

Be the driver of your bus. Don't be a passenger.

The other belief I had instilled in me early on was about working hard and to some extent I agree with it. If you work hard you'll get results. That makes sense, right? But where I went wrong was to think that if I worked harder and harder I'd get increased results. Well I guess that might have worked if I was a machine, but I'm not (and neither are you). We're human and need time to recover and renew. If only I had valued sleep and time out. Both very precious and protected things in my life these days. It's not possible to keep going without breaks and rest. Our bodies and brains need time to recover if you want them to function well.

What would you tell other women who might be experiencing this in their lives?

I wish could I shout from the hill tops so every woman in her 30s could hear. Our bodies are highly sophisticated machines that are capable of incredible feats, but they can only be pushed so far. If you want to have children at some point you need to nurture your body so that it is capable of nurturing another precious life. If you were a gardener and you wanted amazing roses to be blooming next summer, you'd nurture the plant by planting it in the right position, fertilise the soil, make sure it has just the right amount of water, prune it when it was needed and then you could enjoy boundless beautiful blooms. If you genuinely want to be able to have healthy babies, you need to do the same with your body and nurture it to produce its finest crop. Keep your eye on the prize and don't compromise.

The other cliché that is too true to be funny is that 'money doesn't buy you happiness'. Striving for chattels as a symbol of success is a hollow sham and will not bring you the joy you hope for. Of course, you will want to have your basic needs met with a roof over your head (and even a nice one) and food for your family, but don't be fooled. It's not about 'he who has most wins', it's about 'he (or she) who loves life most wins' and money can't buy you that. I believe you only really love life when you appreciate the precious moments you have and the small things like the glint of the snow in the sunshine.

What are some of the things you would have changed about that situation if you could have?

It's fascinating looking back with more wisdom and experience. I wouldn't want to be anywhere else than where I am today, so I guess I wouldn't want to change anything, however, I do regret putting my body through such prolonged levels of chronic stress. I do so wish I had been blessed with more children. My only son, who was conceived naturally when I was 46, wishes it too. I can't believe how much it still hurts.

The other thing I think about is the lasting damage this level of stress has had on my brain and how that might contribute to future mental decline. I am doing everything and anything I can to encourage neurogenesis, and so should you!

Any final words?

Life is short and precious so don't let someone else dictate your life for you. Wake up, take control of the wheel, and enjoy the ride.

How can people get in touch with you and see the work you do?

Sarah@sarahsparks.co.uk
www.sarahsparks.co.uk
Facebook page   - https://www.facebook.com/sarahsparks05/
Facebook group   - https://www.facebook.com/groups/BusyThriveTribe/
For daily tips and techniques about Thriving
LinkedIn - https://www.linkedin.com/in/choose2thrive/

You ARE Worthy – It's Time to Fly.

Hi there! I'm Debbie Cromack and I am the founder of Emerge Empowerment, LLC. I'm an Empowerment and Mindset Coach and I'm passionate about helping female entrepreneurs who are transitioning from corporate jobs to online coaching businesses.

What are you passionate about and how you are contributing to the world?

I have lived through the transition and know how very different the mindset of a successful corporate woman is from the mindset of a success female entrepreneur. Most often, the challenge stems from the mindset that was developed from when we were young. I ignite your empowerment by teaching you how to use the power of your mind to release untruths from your past, blast through your blocks, and illuminate your strengths so you can propel forward with confidence and turn your daunting entrepreneurial journey into a fabulous, blissful business.

Describe a pivotal time in your life you would like to share:

You might think the onset of my panic attacks was a pivotal time for me. While it certainly had me STOP and take a good, hard look at my life, there were more powerful moments that happened long before the panic attacks began that impacted the person I would become and the life I led.

For as far back as I can remember, I have always been creative and liked fashion and decorating and writing...basically things that evoked emotion. I especially enjoyed decorating. The concept of creating a feeling inside someone when they walk into a room. Whether it's the warmth of a cozy living room, ambient romance in a dining room, or the magic of the holiday season, being able to create a feeling brought me joy.

When I was heading to college, like many kids my age, I didn't have any idea what I wanted to major in. While surveying the majors offered at the college I got accepted to, I noticed that they had interior design. Unsure if that would be my path, I was brimming with anticipation. When telling my mother what I was going to study, I excitedly declared, "Interior decorating!"

To which she scoffed and sourly replied, "Debbie, you don't need to go to college to do that."

THUNK. My heart dropped to my feet as my dreams were doused.

There was no discussion. No questions about why I wanted to study interior decorating. No interest in talking any further about it.

I went to my room, depleted. I curled up on my bed and allowed the tears to flow while my head spun.

How could she not see she was breaking my spirit? Stealing my excitement about the possibilities of my future. How could she close her eyes and only see her unrealized dreams? How could she not open her eyes and want to encourage me to go after my dreams, whatever those dreams were?

I remember one day being with my best friend and we were chatting with her parents about college and talking about majors. They encouraged her to study whatever she was interested in. It didn't matter to them what she studied. They just wanted her to be happy and study something that inspired her.

And I remember wondering why my desires weren't encouraged by my parents. Why what I wanted to study wasn't good enough. Why what I wanted to do didn't matter.

I wondered if maybe my dreams were silly and unrealistic. Maybe decorating was not really a career, but just a hobby. Maybe I couldn't make any kind of decent living being an interior decorator. And so, I stuffed away my excitement and numbness filled its place.

I felt confused and lost. No guidance. No interest. No encouragement. I felt alone and unsupported in a scary time of life—going off to college.

Eventually, I figured my mother was right and continued on the path of business and then found that I excelled at psychology, which I ultimately graduated with a degree in.

"Maybe this is a better path for me. Safer for my future." The words floated in my head, but my heart disagreed.

Looking back, what made it such an important part of your life journey?

This moment was an important part of my life's journey because it paved the path of many years of hollowness.

Going off to college and starting my adult life was supposed to be an amazing adventure filled with new discoveries and creating the person I was meant to become. Instead, I pushed my dreams aside and took the 'safe' route.
A route that changed the course of my life.

I followed the path I was supposed to follow. I graduated cum laude, eventually landed in corporate America, and got my MBA. All the while, feeling empty, unfulfilled, and desperately disliking my life.

I didn't feel worthy of going after my dreams. I had very little self-esteem and self-worth. My value and opinion of myself was cemented through my mother's view. What took me a very long time to learn was that those opinions I had formed were actually UN-truths. They did not reflect the person I truly am. But for many years, I thought they did.

Based on the wealth of knowledge, wisdom and experience that you have now, what would you have liked to say to yourself back then?

My dearest Debbie,

Life is filled with things you may not understand. But know there is a reason for everything. And know that when you read this, you are meant to be exactly where you are. Be patient and gentle with yourself... and with others.

There will be a time when your mother will say things to you that you will perceive as you not being worthy and that your dreams aren't important. When you are 5 or 6 years old, she will offer to take you shopping to buy you an outfit. She'll tell you to try on a few outfits to then pick out one she would buy. You will be delighted and excited and try them all on. Once you've narrowed your preferences down to two, you'll ask for her help on the final decision.

You will leave the store with nothing. You will feel sad and not worth the price of one outfit. This will start a pattern of doubting your worth that you won't recognize for many years.

Your self-worth will take another slashing when she squashes your desire to study interior decorating in college. You won't understand why, you will only ache inside. Her scoffing will cut deeper than you realize at the time.

I want you to take a moment to embrace and understand where her words are coming from. She lived in a time when women put their dreams on hold in order to do what society said was "right." She was torn from her quaint little town where her family and friends lived and plopped into a foreign country with three young children to raise. Her white-picket-fenced home and family traditions were destroyed.

And then when the divorce came, her world crashed in around her, crumbling all her dreams of the life she dreamed of.

Open your heart with compassion and know that she came from a time when women didn't pursue their dreams and her words are meant to protect you from the pain of not being able to have your dreams come true.

There will also be a time when your father will do the same thing your mother did and crush your dreams. He will make a decision that you will interpret as your dreams not being important and he will not support you.

While attending college you will do some modelling to feed your creative desires. You will be offered an opportunity to go to New York with a few girls and you will feel thrilled and excited! You will eagerly wonder if this is the opportunity that would be the start of your life's path.

Of course, you needed money to be able to go so you asked your father to pay. You let him know when you needed an answer by and you waited. And you waited.

You will go to the meeting point for the trip with your bags packed and wait with all the other girls. Only you will still be waiting for a call from your father to let you know if he is going to pay for you to be able to go. The girls will load onto the bus...and you will wait. Finally, his call will come.

His answer will be, "No."

You will feel as though someone is squeezing your heart in their fist. As you look up to watch the bus drive away, you feel it pulling with it another of your desires and dreams of your future. You hold your breath and wince, trying to suppress the tears burning behind your eyes. This was a skill you'd become quite good at. You will breathe out in an effort to numb the pain.

Again, I want you to realize that he comes from a time when women were housewives and didn't have dreams except to be mothers and wives, the mould that society deemed appropriate for them. As such, his beliefs tell him that is how you should live your life.

This pattern of stripping away your worth will continue even after college. You will graduate and get your first real job. Knowing you had nothing appropriate to wear as your clothes were all jeans and sweatshirts, your mother will again offer to take you shopping. With a conservative approach, you will select versatile items like a black sheath dress, a black blazer, a skirt, a sweater (on sale for only $20.00!!) and two tops. Before popping out of the fitting room, you will survey your selections.

"Practical, can be mixed and matched...a good start," you will think to yourself.

When you emerge from the fitting room and show her what you settled on, she will take the $20.00 sweater and say, "I'll get you this."

You will feel as though a hammer has smashed your chest, ripping you open.

"I can afford the $20.00 sweater!" you will want to shout.

" If you feel worthless and alone, know you don't have to. Know that you have such incredible power inside you and amazing gifts to share with the world. "

-Debbie Cromack-

As you had become so practiced at, you will choke down a swallow, force back the sting of tears, and graciously say, "Thank you."

Needless to say, your self-worth will take yet another of many blows.

I know you will feel angry and bitter and unworthy of your desires. See life as they lived it and simply understand. Parenting comes with no book to tell you exactly what to do. Parents, parent through what they know and their life experiences. They often parent through fear, protection, and their own demons.

And when your mother attempts suicide twice, you will learn that when your dreams have been broken, you become broken. You will learn to abolish your dreams and give up on life, give up on your family. You will see yourself as unworthy and your dreams as unimportant.

You will feel lost and broken for more than 25 years of your adulthood. And you will feel abandoned at times when you most wanted and needed to feel supported and encouraged. You will do what you thought you were supposed to do instead of what you are meant to do. And you will feel anger, frustration, resentment. You will feel a calling to follow your dreams and you will deny that calling because you will allow your ego, your fears, to hold you back.

You will make bad financial decisions in an effort to fill the emptiness, the void. You will mistakenly think that if you buy pretty clothes and shoes and jewellery, you will look good enough, feel good enough, be good enough. You will spend money on things that make you feel momentarily happy and then leave your soul still barren.

And those bad decisions will haunt you while leaving you still vacant of worth. You will battle a mountain of insurmountable debt for the better part of those 25 years that will lead into your mid-40s, and you will fear living a frightening future as you get old because you will not have saved any money in order to survive.

I want you to have no regrets. Why, you wonder? Because every bit of your journey is an essential part of your ultimate transformation into the magnificent woman you will become.

The pain you feel will allow you to know the pain of the women you will work with one day and it will give you compassion. The sorrow of having your dreams quenched at every turn will help you to know the anguish they feel. The emptiness in your heart that your dreams don't matter, that you don't matter, will enhance your understanding of the hollowness they feel so you can support them from a place of knowing.

Know that you are worthy and that your dreams are important. Know that you were put on this earth to make a healthy, positive impact on the lives of women. And the only way for you to do that is to follow your journey exactly as you are. Embrace the pain and let it be your teacher.

Never give up on your dreams. Know that they may not come in the timing or package you want. Stay resilient and know that your path will guide you to your happiness

.
Learn to be grateful for all that you have rather than disappointed about what you don't have. Learn to cherish precious moments and hold their memories in your mind for when the day has dragged you down. Learn to honour the heartaches and difficulties in life and always take away a lesson or opportunity to grow.

Trust God, trust yourself, and trust your journey. Follow your heart and let your intuition guide you. Allow your desire for a happy, fulfilling life to empower you to create it. Your purpose will reveal itself when you are ready to fulfil it.

You are worthy. Your dreams are important. Be patient and gentle with yourself. Know that you have a purpose and you will create the life you desire and are worthy of.

All my love,

Debbie

How did this event change your life?

My pivotal moment changed my life because it provided me with the insight I would need to someday help women whose lives are similarly parallel mine, so I can understand their darkness and be able to help them ignite the power inside themselves, so they can experience their own transformation.

What golden nuggets did you learn from this experience?

I learned the power of words and the impact they have on others regardless of our intentions. I learned that, while the message may be well-meaning, the pain of feeling worthless can be piercing and take a long time to heal. I learned that my emotional scars can be my strength and not just my weakness. I am not a victim, rather I am a warrior with a message and a purpose to support women in fulfilling their dreams while fulfilling mine simultaneously.

Ultimately, we make our dreams come true and we should not allow others to dictate our dreams or our path.

It's never too late to go after your dreams. I was in my mid-40s when I had my first panic attack. I had no idea what was happening to me and thought I was dying. Intense, irrational fear filled me, my outer body tremored while my insides vibrated, sweat draped my skin, a strange claustrophobia suffocated me, and my heart beat wildly in my chest.

After a series of these attacks and being put on an anti-anxiety medicine that made it hard for me to breathe, I decided I had had ENOUGH.

I was stressed beyond belief, working 12-14 hours a day (and sometimes working on weekends) at a job I despised. I was exhausted and unhappy to the point that I cried almost every other day. I was unfulfilled and had no sense of purpose. I was empty and tired of the numbness that I had used to cope.

I did a lot of soul-searching during that time. I looked back on my life to figure out how I had gotten to such a destitute place.

And I discovered a lot about the patterns I had adopted as normal. It was during this time that I decided I was no longer going to live that way and I was going to help other women stop living lives they loathed and start living the lives they are meant to live.

What are some of the things you would have changed about that situation if you could have?

Would I change anything if I could? Absolutely not. Everything we experience in our lives has an important part of creating the person we are. How we choose to perceive those experiences and what we choose to do with what we learn is in our control. I could have let my lack of self-worth continue to keep me trapped in a miserable existence. Instead, I used it to fuel my purpose and create a life of value and happiness, so I can help other women find their empowerment, spread their wings, and fly.

What would you tell other women who might be experiencing this in their lives?

If you feel worthless and alone, know you don't have to. Know that you have such incredible power inside you and amazing gifts to share with the world. Know that you have a purpose and it's time to live it. Coming out of that dark place is not easy, but I can assure you it's so worth it...and so are you. Give yourself permission to step away from what your parents, society and your loved ones say you "should" do and step into what your heart's desire is calling out to you to do.

I encourage you to work with a coach. Find someone whose story resonates with you and whose vibe is energetically aligned with you. You don't have to go through anything alone. One of my sayings is, "Girls, we are so much better and stronger TOGETHER." We need each other in this world. Let's help one another create the fabulous lives we are meant to live!

Any final words?

If you don't believe in you, know that I believe in you. My purpose is to help you do what you want to do, what you are meant to do, regardless of what is societally acceptable.

Believe in the person you are becoming.

You matter, and your dreams are important. It's time to claim your power!

How can people get in touch with you and see the work you do?

I'd love to connect with you. Here's where you can find me.
Email: Debbie@EmergeEmpowerment.com
Website: www.EmergeEmpowerment.com
Facebook:
https://www.facebook.com/emergeempower/(@EmergeEmpower)

The Story of the Life Liberator

I am Ruth Driscoll, founder of The Life Liberator. And I'm on a mission!

What are you passionate about and how you are contributing to the world?

I am creating a global liberation, leading women out of manipulative, abusive and controlling relationships into empowerment and freedom.

I believe that every woman is entitled to create a destiny that gives her the confidence to be herself and to live her life with happiness, fulfilment and positivity. That way she is able to contribute to building happiness and peace in our world.

Imagine a world where 10,000,000 or more abused women regain their lives, free from bullying and control. Can it be done? I believe so. And that is where I am setting my intention and my contribution.

It takes only the smallest stone dropped into a pond to create a ripple that builds in size, intensity and reach. From one small action, the result can be extraordinary.

Describe a pivotal time in your life you would like to share.

Have you ever wondered how it feels to live inside an abusive relationship? I hope that it is something you never get to experience. I, unfortunately, do know.

That was my world. A strange, bewildering, irrational place where your spirit is constantly consumed by your own edgy nervousness. You will have heard that expression 'treading on egg-shells.' That was how I spent my life. Imagine living with the continual confusion of inexplicable episodes of cruelty that leave you feeling bereft, inadequate and hopeless. Then without explanation, all is loving again! But it's a calm that you daren't trust because it can vanish as swiftly and as bewilderingly as it arrived.

You find yourself doing whatever it takes to try and maintain the calm, to stop things from 'kicking off.' And with all the energy that drains from you, it means that the one person you have no time for is yourself. You dare not allow your emotions to show. It's like you take up a smaller and smaller space inside your own life.

The impact of that is that you completely lose who you are.

No wonder those living in abusive relationships often feel like they are going mad!

It was only when I finally realised that everything that came out of his mouth was in some way twisted, manipulated or exaggerated that I felt I could actually trust my own judgement. Maybe I wasn't going mad after all! Trying to use logic to rationalise his rantings and his accusations was like trying to create a Ming vase out of house bricks.

Looking back, I can see that at my darkest time I felt that I didn't want to live any more. Though, oddly, that doesn't mean I was suicidal. I definitely wasn't. I guess I just felt that living had become too painful and too exhausting. I suppose I had given up hope.

There are those times in your life when you need to draw on the depths of your inner resources. We know that the only way something can change is if we do something differently. But, oh boy! Sometimes it can take a while for that to really sink in.

See, I knew all that stuff! At this time, I was the head teacher of a challenging inner-city primary school. I dealt with difficult situations every day. Wasn't that just what I did - supporting others to do things differently and get a better result - every day?!

I was a qualified life coach. I used these skills to great effectiveness within my job.

My life was this crazy dichotomy of being a respected and valued leader in the community to being this 'other' person. Who the heck was she?! That someone whose only role was seemingly to please and pander to 'his' every whim. Now I look back with the wisdom of hindsight; that's how it appears. It's very easy to feel ashamed of yourself. That means it's not easy for you to talk about what you're living through with anybody else. It also means that you don't admit to yourself that you're in an abusive relationship.

I'm pleased to say that the day came when I did do something differently. From somewhere I found the strength even at the point where I felt it had all been drained out of me. I chucked him out.

A momentous day? Looking back on it, yes. But, at the time? No.

Initially my life dipped into a place of even greater strain. I didn't know then that the bullying gets worse once the abuser feels they have lost control of you. Plus, you are also dealing with your own massive emotional fall-out and a complete readjustment of your life.

My health suffered very badly, ultimately putting me in a hospital bed. I lay in that bed wondering if I would ever get better. Yet, this was the pivotal moment that sent my life on a completely new path.

When something has crumbled to dust, the only option is to rebuild.

When I came out of hospital I had to relearn how to eat. I had to relearn how to walk. Most importantly, I had to relearn how to be me again.

Who was Ruth Driscoll before she lost herself?

I set off on a journey of recovery and discovery.

I had to look back, way back, to try and understand how this could have happened to me. And what did I have to learn? What did I have to do to make sure this could never happen to me again? Is this a situation that could have been averted? How far back do I need to travel to speak to the younger me, so I know why I was vulnerable to manipulation, bullying and control.

Based on the wealth of knowledge, wisdom and experience that you have now, what would you have liked to say to yourself back then?

Dear Ruth,

It's odd, the things that stick in our minds, isn't it?

Do you remember that day? You're about eight years old, with long plaited hair bobbing on your back as you're walking to school with the gang of other children. You've learned to do that funny thing with your eyes. You know, that thing that means you can see two of everything. It's kind of fun, isn't it?

Of course, you don't realise that what you're actually doing is going cross-eyed. So, in fact, everyone else can see what you're doing.

That's why it's a bit of a shock when that boy says to you in his strong Cardiff accent, with a look of admiration on his face, "Aww! 'Ow d'you do tha'?"

There is a reason why that trivial and momentary incident will stay in your mind. The things that remain in our minds from our childhood days are often those moments of significant emotional importance. I know now why that moment holds significance. It is the first time that you realise that you can do something that maybe others can't do.

Of course, there are lots of things that you can do - and do really well - that maybe others can't. It's just that you have no concept of that yet because right now your image of yourself is that you are just very ordinary. Well, not even ordinary but rather unimportant. You have the belief that if you can do something, it means that everyone else can. There's nothing special about you.

You haven't really ever heard much in the way of praise. Though you are pretty clear that you're not good at very much.

As your mother often says, "You're more trouble to me now than when you were a baby." So, I guess the message is that you were a troublesome baby and it would appear that you haven't managed to make much improvement. It's just that you're not quite sure what it is that you're doing that's so troublesome. What if you just try harder to please her? Maybe that will stop her looking so cross all the time. I wonder if that will work. Maybe that will mean that you can avoid those days when she doesn't speak to you at all and the air is frosty with disapproval. But it's hard to know how to put something right when you don't even know what's wrong.

You even asked Father Christmas for a real magic wand, so you could magic away all her housework. That was such a brilliant idea, wasn't it! But I don't think Father Christmas could do that. I think that might be why he looked a bit worried and spoke quietly to your daddy. So that plan didn't work!

But what if it's just because you're there? Just by being there, by being you, you're doing the wrong thing and you're upsetting her. That doesn't seem very easy to put right. But it must be that! And it makes you feel really bad about who you are.

Perhaps that's why, on that day walking to school, that boy's expression of admiration is stirring a feeling inside you that you've never experienced before. And you don't really know how to describe it. Then when the rest of the gang crowd around so you can teach them how to go cross-eyed too, there's that fleeting moment you realise that you're doing something that others can't and that those others want to find out about it so they can do it too. It's only, of course, years later that you realise why you remember that day.

What you do know is that, to a little girl who doesn't feel she has anything to offer, it feels nice.

The writer, Albert Camus, states, '... good intentions may do as much harm as malevolence if they lack understanding.'

You certainly don't feel it right now, but your mother did love you. Everything she ever did was intended for your benefit. You know the sacrifices that were made to ensure you and your brother and sister had opportunities that she never enjoyed.

But we have to be careful what we pass on to our children. If we're not conscious of that, then it can take generations to work through the damage caused by a negative and oppressive upbringing. It's hard for a child to grow up with confidence when they only know about where they are failing. It's hard, in those circumstances, for a child to grow up loving herself. I know that now.

Let's take a quick glance at your mother's life so we can understand better how the only way she could show her love was through a control born of anxiety; through an inability to communicate effectively; through her own upbringing that crushed her means of expressing herself.

There are values of resilience and determination in the 'stiff upper lip' generation. Life was tough. Nobody had much. What you did have you shared. And you never let anyone else know the extent of your struggles.

Your grandmother was widowed when your mother was four years old. There was no benefit system to help you out in those days, so you just did what you could to survive and pride was paramount. You certainly didn't let your emotions show. That meant you didn't complain and you definitely didn't demand or expect anything.

Your mother learned that when your coat became worn and tatty there wasn't money for a new one. So, what could you do? Well, you unpicked that coat, turned the pieces around so the inner fabric was now on the outside. Then you sewed the pieces back up again adding a new lining. If a jumper got worn out at the elbow, you unpicked the wool until it passed the worn bit. Then you re-knitted it with any good wool from the unpicking and added a band in a contrasting colour to the lower sleeve.

To the outside world it looked like a new jumper or a new coat. Covering up your poverty was a labour-intensive and proud operation. It seems incredible in today's world that so much effort would go into maintaining your standards.

" I believe that every woman is entitled to create a destiny that gives her the confidence to be herself and to live her life with happiness, fulfilment and positivity. That way she is able to contribute to building happiness and peace in our world. "

-Ruth Driscoll-

In a world where every day is a struggle, sentimentality becomes a luxury that you can't afford to indulge. There's no time for fun or frivolity. You put on your stiff upper lip, button in your emotions and press forward.

When she was a young girl there was a brief moment of huge excitement. Affluent relatives who lived in Scotland sent two glorious party dresses - one for her and one for her older sister. Frothy, frilly, completely impractical... and just perfect! Every little girl's dream!

Those dresses were never once worn, never even tried on. They never left their boxes. And all the longing of that little girl to put on that dress and, just once feel like a princess, had to be squashed and hidden deep inside. Don't complain. Don't demand. Don't. Even. Ask!

What might that relentless lack of an outlet for joyful expression do to a young mind?

Ruth, if you come and stand here with me now, you will see how that uncompromising childhood crushed so much of who your mother could have been. It crushed joy and spontaneity and opened the doors to anxiety, duty and oppressive responsibility, yet it also created a woman of determination, resilience and strong values. And, more than that, a woman of inspiration! You can feel justly proud that she is your mother. Yet, as we look back, like me, you will feel the overwhelming sadness for the chances that she never had to fully be who she could have been. The opportunity to be loved by her children that she never allowed to flourish. The fear that we would become 'spoiled' by displays of affection.

You will understand why, as you become a teenager and a young woman, you felt that overwhelming need to throw off that suffocating and oppressive disapproval of everything you did and why you felt such a need to escape!

It was the only way that you could be you.

You will understand why, through all the years that followed, you never turned to your mother to seek advice or to confide in her.

And you will again feel such sadness that it was another element of contribution and connection that was denied to her.

You will feel sadness that she never understood why the oppression and hardship of her own upbringing manifested in passive-aggressive behaviour towards those closest to her. I'm sure she never understood the harm it did. Her motive was to be certain you didn't grow up 'big-headed'! Understand that she believed she was doing the best for you to be an upright and responsible person. In her world that meant that love and affection were weaknesses. You had to keep your stiff upper lip. But that's why you couldn't grow up feeling sure that you were loved; you couldn't feel confident of who you were and comfortable with the talents and abilities that you possessed.

To find those things you must make that journey for yourself. And remember that each time you feel that you have failed, each time you feel that you've made a mess of it, there's a lesson to be learned that will help you to grow and to be proud of who you will become.

You will learn your toughest and most effective lessons when you become involved with that abusive man. This is where you will need to confront the conditioning from your upbringing that caused you to easily accept the negative messages about yourself that he hurled at you. You will recognise why you were vulnerable to his manipulation and control. But it's also where you will examine who you truly are, how you can undo the damage caused by that early conditioning and finally learn to love yourself.

Oh, and you won't need to go cross-eyed to achieve it!

With all my love

Ruth, the Older Me.

How did this event change your life?

This quote from Maya Angelou helps me to rationalise my conflicting feelings towards my mother: "I've learned that people will forget what you said, people will forget what you did, but people will never forget how you made them feel."

So, yes, I had tough lessons to learn. As I recovered physically, mentally and emotionally from my time spent living with an abusive partner, these lessons had to release me from the damaging beliefs I held about myself.

Do you find that sometimes the important realisations you have in life come almost as though someone suddenly switched on a light in a dark tunnel or as if the universe had sent a thunderbolt electrifying your brain? Those flashing moments of insight can change your beliefs and alter the path of your destiny.

What golden nuggets did you learn from this experience?

The first happened quite soon after my abusive relationship had ended. I know now that, so often, women in abusive relationships keep quiet about what is going on behind closed doors. (Oh! So, it wasn't just me!) But I was in such turmoil that I needed to talk. He was gone. There was nothing to cover up any longer. I spoke with a close friend and told her what I had been dealing with. The words she said to me came like that thunderbolt of realisation.

"Ruth," she said, "How could you let this happen to you?"

Think about how she expressed those words. She didn't say, 'How could this have happened!' The thunderbolt words are 'you let this happen.' Whoa! I realised she was right. Somehow, though completely unconsciously, I had let this happen to me. Over the years I had done very little to protect myself. I didn't know how to stand my ground.

Anyone living with an abusive relationship knows it's far more complex than just a simple realisation. But it's a great start to the change of mind-set needed to overcome an abusive situation.

This understanding can benefit anyone no matter what their situation. Ask yourself this question. What is happening in your life that you are letting happen to you? Or who do you know who is letting something happen to them? You may find it's surprisingly commonplace when you start asking that question.

The younger me believed that I should accept and be tolerant. Surely, I would have said, if you love someone enough it will all work out alright in the end? So long as you're a good girl and do as you're told; so long as you don't make any fuss, then things will be alright, won't they?

Of course, now I know that I did not have boundaries in place to protect myself from the unacceptable behaviour of others.

'Letting it happen' indicates passivity. Ask yourself, "What action am I taking?"

You have to be active. Take the controls on your own life.

Another thunderbolt struck while I was lying in my hospital bed. I lay there, drifting in and out of sleep. Though my brain was foggy, it was still telling me insistently that I had to make radical changes to the way I was living my life. I had to release myself from stress in order to stay healthy. But how? At that time, it felt like there were things that I couldn't escape from, obligations which I had to fulfil.

Often the reason you can't move forward in life is because you are holding on to something in the past. Something that no longer serves you. Something that you can't change.

The younger me believed that I couldn't let anyone down. If someone needed help, it was my duty to be there for them. I would push aside my own needs to attend to those of others. The message from my childhood that I was unimportant coloured my approach to my obligation towards others in my life. Shoving aside my own needs to be there for others was my default setting.

I would never want to lose that quality of being there for others. I believe it's a great way to be. But it should work in a reciprocal way.

It's when it tips over into allowing yourself to be taken advantage of by the unscrupulous that it becomes a problem and not a quality.

This quotation has helped me to find balance when I feel myself heading towards serving others when it is not justified:

'Grant me the courage to change the things I can; the serenity to accept the things I can't; and the wisdom to know the difference.'

What would you tell other women who might be experiencing this in their lives?

My warning is to be cautious of the demands of duty and obligation. Make sure the balance isn't being tipped too far in a direction that compromises you.

This is a simple but powerful exercise that I devised to help my clients get a greater sense of how duty and obligation may be creating stress in their lives. Maybe you could try it out now for yourself.

Get a pen and paper and write down all of the qualities you possess. Write each one as a short sentence.

So, for example, you might write, "I am kind." "I am tolerant." "I am generous." Make this list as long as you can, honestly and without modesty!
When you look at that list, you should feel justly proud of the wonderful qualities that you offer. These are qualities for which you should be valued and cherished by those around you.

But now I'm going to ask you to make one tiny change to each of those sentences which will completely change the meaning of that sentence. To each sentence, add the word "too."

For example, "I am too kind."

See how the picture that is now painted shows how you may be sabotaging yourself. Reflect on where that word "too" applies to you. Ask yourself what effect that is having on your life.

I call this 'Too Syndrome.' When your sense of duty and obligation to others may be overwhelming you, consider how you can reverse the effects of 'Too Syndrome' so you can still maintain the qualities that make you who you are but stop you from being taken advantage of.

What are some of the things you would have changed about that situation if you could have?

It seems odd that, so often, you hear from someone who has been through adversity, they say that, although it was horrendous at the time, they are glad that they went through it. I believe that the reason people feel that way is because they recognise how that experience forced them to grow as a person and they discovered greater depths to their own essential core. They discover resourcefulness within themselves that might never have been uncovered.

Of course, I wish I'd never met him. I wish I hadn't wasted years of my time and squandered my love on him. But, weirdly, I don't regret that it happened. Because of my experience, I have now plugged the gaps inside myself that would otherwise have continued to leave me vulnerable and puzzled about why that was so. I am so much more confident about my strength and resilience. I've been tested, and I've come through to the other side. I am so much more self-reliant.

Strangely, if this abusive situation had never happened to me, I would still be the head teacher of that inner-city primary school. Making the decision to resign was very tough. I had to fight the guilt that decision made me feel. How could I let down that whole community? It was probably one of the few times that I put my own needs first! And, boy, did I struggle with it! Overcoming undeserved guilt is an important part of protecting yourself. The quality of life that I now enjoy is vastly superior. And I don't just mean for me only!

As an entrepreneur running my own business, I now use my time in a way that gives me greater balance in my life. I can use my skills to impact and positively influence a worldwide community. My reach is far greater. I would never have believed that possible about myself and may never have explored the ways in which I can contribute to the world.

Adversity can either cause you to shrink or to grow. Michelle Obama describes it far more eloquently than I. "You should never view your challenges as a disadvantage. Instead, it's important for you to understand that your experience facing and overcoming adversity is actually one of your biggest advantages."

That's such a great way to think. Of course, it's not so easy to do that when you're going through it. But the examples are there from so many people who went through the pain and came out the other side stronger, calmer and more empowered than before.

I can truly say that, for me, everything has changed for the better. On a personal level, I am in the privileged place of having time to spend with my family and friends. The most important and wonderful part of this is that I now have two little grandsons. And I've been able to spend lots of time with them and build a really close bond. I also have a brand new little granddaughter. I feel the wisdom I can offer them coupled with unconditional love is so much stronger because of the journey I've undertaken to learn from my experience and keep improving.

Any final words?

I've learned to trust the road that the Universe puts me on. I believe that She gives you the experience you require to learn the valuable lesson that you need to become an even better and more successful version of yourself.
And along the way, I realised that this is why I am here. You could say I discovered my purpose. If this could happen to me, it could happen to anyone. And because of my background and experience, I am perfectly placed to help others to overcome their abusive situation and regain their lives.

Finally, at last, I can say, 'Ruth, I love you!'

How can people get in touch with you and see the work you do?
ruth@thelifeliberator.org
www.thelifeliberator.org

Refined by Fire

Debby Montgomery Johnson, founder of The Woman Behind the Smile movement, Radio Show Host, International Speaker, Best-Selling Author

What are you passionate about and how you are contributing to the world?

I am the woman behind the global movement for women to recognize and own up to their unique hidden story – a story that may be silently held by many others but not shared.

Describe a pivotal time in your life you would like to choose.

So many times could be classified as 'pivotal' in my life – choosing THE ONE for this project is daunting. My most public moment to date was when I was scammed for over $1 million in an online dating relationship. I talk about this a lot in my book, The Woman Behind the Smile – Triumph Over the Ultimate Online Dating Betrayal. What pivotal time in my life prior to that led me to being vulnerable to be taken so completely?

I'm going to take you back to Woodstock, Vermont, January 1974. I was just 15 years old and was packing up to go away to boarding school for the first time. I was so excited to be going off to Philips Exeter Academy, one of the most prestigious secondary schools in the US! Although I was scared to leave home for the first time without my family, I was thrilled at the thought of new friends, great sports teams, and an academic challenge (was that my idea or my parents'?!) Exeter had a beautiful campus with brick dormitories and classrooms, a magnificent library, and a state of the art physical education facility and acres of playing fields – it was a college prep campus and those attending were college-bound. The competition was fierce, and I was honoured to be accepted to the school mid-sophomore year.

Two weeks before leaving for Exeter my idyllic life was shattered by 'The Fire' – I'm going to have my dad (Dr. Jack Butz, author of My 50 Golden Years) tell this part of the story. Although the fire of Pine View 1 was the first devastating and pivotal event in my life, I came into the story after the fact. I was at a church event with my younger brothers and was picked up by a friend's mom only to find out what had happened during the previous few hours.

"January 18, 1974. It was a typically frigid day, with temperatures reaching minus five degrees Fahrenheit, when I arrived home for dinner from the office. It was pleasant since the memories of the Christmas holiday were still fresh and some decorations were still scattered throughout the house. The house was filled with the odour of the soon to be served dinner. Then, as Gwen gave me a greeting kiss, she calmly told me that she had had difficulty getting our relatively new station wagon started today because it was so cold. I turned and went directly to the garage that I had just parked my Jeep in, next to my garden tractor that now served as a snow blower. After a few tries I was able to get the wagon started and I laid a brick on the accelerator pedal, in order to keep the engine running at a speed that would soon recharge the battery. This was an operation that I had performed a multitude of times on cold days. I noticed the smell of gasoline, but that was normal when a car has been flooded in the starting process. With task completed I returned to the house through a breezeway that connected the garage to the house and left the car purring in the garage."

My parents were in the process of completely redecorating the first floor of the house and our large dining room had many of my great-grandfather's precious books, paintings, and trophies spread out on the dining room table, so the family had to eat meals downstairs in the basement family room.

"At approximately 8:00 p.m., the room suddenly became pitch dark, and it was evident that we had lost our electricity, but why? I moved around to look out of our small basement window and observed that the entire outside area was lit up with shades of orange and red that were very ominous. Gwen and I raced upstairs to the kitchen and to the back door only to experience the shock of seeing the garage in flames which nearly overpowered us. Because we had lost electricity and had no phone service we were unable to report the fire to the local fire station, so we ran away from the house to get a neighbour to call. I stepped in front of the garage and wanted to quickly get into my Jeep, which might be saved from its burning garage mate. Gwen, however, grabbed me and said, "I love you and you are NOT going in there!" Discretion taking over I decided she was right, so we raced down the driveway and within seconds a fiery explosion took what was left of the station wagon and engulfed the little Jeep, along with my beautiful International Harvester tractor in flames. Gwen was right again, and I was thankful for her good sense — what are wives for, eh?? I can always buy another 4-wheeler!"

Fathers – wow! At this point our family was changed forever. Our world and all of our worldly things were either consumed by, or damaged by fire, water and smoke, or so it seemed at the time.

Looking back what made it such an important part of your life journey?

The fire for me was a lesson in finding out what was truly important. Yes, I had all of my new clothes, stuffed animals, pillows, books, and sports equipment out ready to be packed up for my move to PEA. My life was about to change, and my emotions were on the edge and my belongings were completely ruined. Our beautiful home was now dripping with stained water and things were either charred or covered in soot and ash, and I'll NEVER forget the smell of smoke for the rest of my life. I cried for our loss. I cried because I saw my mom and dad crying because everything they worked for and provided for my brothers and me was physically gone. However, the most important part of the fire was not the loss of stuff, but that I came to recognize the value of family and service. No one was hurt in the fire except for my sweet Powder, my beautiful, longhaired angora kitty, who died of smoke inhalation the day after the fire. I saw first-hand the value of service, and a community coming together to help us clean up without any thought of remuneration. I learned that all our worldly possessions were just that—stuff—nice to have but totally unnecessary in living a truly meaningful life.

When I got to Exeter I was dropped off rather quickly in a new environment with no one around that I knew and everything new in my suitcase. Although my new roommates and teachers were friendly and kind, I felt like a little fish in a very big ocean and sharks were circling – some were nurse sharks, and some felt like big whites! I was an A student back home, excelling in academics, sports, and music. At Exeter I was one of thousands who were 'just like me' but now half of us were going to be at the bottom of the class—a first for me. I struggled with math and science initially so gone was my dream of being an anaesthesiologist! I worked hard in English, music, and French classes and earned my way onto the squash and tennis teams. Classes were six days a week with sports events on Wednesday and Saturday afternoons, so I rarely got home to see my parents. I missed them terribly but didn't feel I could express those feelings for fear of not doing my part or being strong enough in the face of adversity. I knew they were still struggling with getting the house cleaned up and repaired so there would be a home to come back to in May. I had to 'man up' and get my grades up because my competitive side was dying with the 'failures'.

I fell in love for the very first time with a terrific young man from Massachusetts. Although I say today that I really didn't like dating when I was young, our relationship was the closest thing to being home and I clung to it with all my heart and soul. He was a year older than I and had some of the same struggles with academics that I had but we rarely talked about those. We took long walks and had long talks, and when possible, we went to his parent's home for part of the weekends just to get away from the pressures we felt at school. I was very sensitive about my looks – was I as pretty as my roomies? I didn't think so. Was I as smart as my other girlfriends? I didn't think so. But when I was with him it didn't matter. I was important to him and that made me feel good. However, he did say once that I looked better in a skirt than jeans, so for about 30 years after we broke up I didn't wear jeans! Either he was a 'leg man' or I just didn't know how to pick out a good pair of jeans. We helped each other through a challenging time in our youth and we had many 'defining moments' and pivotal experiences together – another book's worth!

My experience with the fire and with going away to Exeter taught me to be strong and to jump into new experiences. I learned to adapt and to be tenacious in my striving for excellence. I was determined to get to the top of the class by the end of my senior year. I made the Principal's Honour Role and I accepted that I didn't have to be #1 there as long as I had been kind, hard-working, and of service to another. I sometimes put myself into situations where I felt like I wasn't enough, but I now know that's just a limiting belief and not reality. I know that I am enough because I'm a daughter of God and I was put on this earth for a divine reason and my experiences in life have given me what I needed to succeed.

Based on the wealth of knowledge, wisdom and experience that you have now, what would you have liked to say to yourself back then?

Dear Debby,

Wow, you've certainly had a lifetime of incredible experiences – the good, the bad, and the necessary! What a strong woman you have become and what an example of goodness, grace and resilience you are to women around the world today.

If I were talking to you back at Exeter, I never would have seen you then as you are now, so I want you to LISTEN UP! I want you to remember you are truly a young woman of divine nature and worth. Not only are you precious to your mom and dad – and no, they didn't get to know your hometown girlfriend better than you just because you went away to school – but you are precious to all you come in contact with. You have a special gift of listening with your heart. You have the power and grace to comfort another in their time of need or pain in spite of your own grief or insecurities.

Remember to talk about your feelings – don't 'stuff them' in order to appear in control. Many will call on you and will call you "a strong woman" and I want you to believe them, but don't shut off your feelings in order to be strong in the sight of others. Being vulnerable isn't a sign of weakness and, in fact, it's the thing that others will be drawn to you for as you grow up.

Think kindly of yourself as you look in the mirror. You have beautiful, long, brown hair that is special to the men in your life, but it frames a beautiful and genuinely kind face. Your dark brown eyes can pierce the soul of others but the special glint in them draws them in and showers them with your love. You feel you are a 'big girl' in stature and others say you've got big, athletic bones and that may be true, but your outside doesn't define your inside! You can, and will, gain and lose weight over the years and you'll find a body type that fits you one day. Work hard at seeing inner beauty and it will reflect your outer beauty. You will be lovelier as you grow older because you will be more accepting of yourself then. Wear jeans if you want to...you may hear others' remarks but STAND UP and be TRUE TO YOU and do what you want, not what others want for you.

Always surround yourself with good people – those who are honest, full of integrity, kind, helpful, and filled with spirit. Life is about relationships, not things, and you learned that because of the fire.

Debby, my dear, hold true to your standards. You were taught well, and you know how valuable you are. Don't do what others might be doing if you feel it might compromise your beliefs. Learn all you can through study, travel, experiences and good people, yet hold on to your internal compass, for it will guide you for good.

Take more risks as you get older. Jump off that high pole and grasp the trapeze once you assess the security and the dangers. You tend to assess things and sometimes you miss out on living – LOVE, LIVE, LEAD, and with that, JUMP into a life that you'll be proud of. Know that throughout your life you'll feel love, deep sadness, and great joy. All experiences will be for your good if you believe that things happen for a reason.

Find the reason and the good in all situations and when you're in the middle of something fearful, sad, or scary, go through it quickly. Don't wallow in self-pity and shame. Like you learned early in life – 'man up' and move forward. Your experiences will help another one day, and your joy will be in seeing others JUMP!

Debby, use your physical and mental strength for your good, and keep healthy. You'll find joy in being able to walk, run, swim and play with your grandchildren one day! Your health is precious. Too many take it for granted and then one day find they don't have it.

Be mindful of your eating habits and take all things in moderation. Be happy in your body – others will tell you that you're too skinny, or too heavy...you'll feel like there is no winning, but you'll know what's perfect for you. Don't let the mirror of your past keep you from seeing your present and future beauty.

Like the airline attendants tell us, "If traveling with others, put on your own oxygen mask before helping others." Your well must be filled before you can give of yourself to others. You will need to learn how to gently say "No" to others lest you take on too many projects.

Doing everything for everyone else keeps them from the blessing of doing things for themselves!

Teach and live self-reliance and prepare for your every needful thing. You will find your reward in heaven if you don't see it here on earth!

So, today, as I write back to the young woman who was dropped off in a scary, exciting, wonderful experience, I say to you, "Embrace the challenge."

"Remember to talk about your feelings – don't "stuff them" in order to appear in control"

Debby Montgomery Johnson

Share your feelings as you grow up so you can lift up another going through similar experiences. STAND UP in our power and grace and be the voice of an articulate, smart, kind, compassionate woman. The world is looking to you as a leader. Lead with love and elevate another as you go forward.

Hugs, my dearest.

What golden nuggets did you learn from this experience?

Life as I see it has its peaks and valleys. The peaks are exciting and provide some of the most fun, happy memories, yet the valleys provide the most impact, possibility of pain, and opportunities for learning and growth. Control and perfectionism tell us to stay in a box where we feel comfortable. They tell us to manipulate our environments, so we never feel vulnerable, needy or uncertain. They keep us safe from our fears of failing, embarrassment and rejection, and sadly, we miss out on a lot of life because of them. As I write this piece, my control buttons are just screaming and the grip of procrastination is crushing me. Perhaps I feel vulnerable opening up another pivotal moment in my life because my 'defining moments' are out in the public for all to hear, see, and comment on. My most vulnerable times are being sliced and diced so others can learn from what I went through and that's very important, yet somewhat uncomfortable, for me.

What would you tell other women who might be experiencing this in their lives?

Learn from your experiences and stand up for yourself no matter what. Be mindful of what others want from you and be kind but don't give away the farm just because others want something from you. Family is so important and, for me, friends fall into that category. But not everyone is your friend and I had to learn that the hard way. I was taken advantage of by several people in my life but going back to learning that stuff isn't everything in life – I live by the saying, "Our last suit has no pockets," and I'm not going to take anything physical with me, but I will take my experiences, my loves, and my knowledge with me and those are the most important. Do your due diligence in business transactions and be mindful of your resources. Always take care of yourself before giving to others – don't forget your own oxygen mask!

What are some of the things you would have changed about that situation if you could have?

I don't really believe that you should change things that have happened in your life because there is a lesson in everything. I would have wanted to spare my family the hurt of losing our home and all of the precious family treasures, but you can't take those things with you. I learned by going away to school that I didn't want my children to go away from me during their formative years – again FAMILY is FOREVER and so important to me! I believe my experiences have moulded me into the woman I am today – one that finally recognizes her worth and potential to do good.

Any final words?

Believe in yourself. Treasure the people in your life and learn from their experiences so you don't have to experience everything for yourself! Speak up so others can learn from you and CTR – Choose the Right. I've learned to LOVE again, and life is good, truly good, because of my good, bad and necessary!

How can people get in touch with you and see the work you do?

www.TheWomanBehindTheSmile.com
https://www.facebook.com/TheWomanBehindTheSmile/
https://www.linkedin.com/in/debbybutzmontgomery/
Debby@TheWomanBehindTheSmile.com
http://bit.ly/womanbehindsmile
https://www.amazon.com/My-50-Golden-Years-Retrievers/dp/1436354927/
ref=sr_1_5?ie=UTF8&qid=1507408645&sr=8-5&keywords=jack+butz

When Your World Comes Crashing Down

My name is Leeanne Lowe, owner and CEO of Empire Creative Marketing.

What are you passionate about and how you are contributing to the world?

My mission is to help others discover their authentic purpose and inspire them on their journey to success in accomplishing their goals. On a professional level, this means helping my clients communicate their brands effectively, and leading a team of creative professionals in developing attractive and engaging marketing campaigns to support them. On a personal level, this means being a loving and supportive mother, daughter, sister, and friend who listens and encourages those I love.

Describe a pivotal time in your life that you would like to share.

At seventeen years old, I thought I had it all. I was graduating a year early, one of the top in my class with a scholarship to attend Arizona State University. I was engaged to marry my high school sweetheart, whom I was deeply in love with. I had a great family, true love, a good job, school covered - I had it all figured out and I was on top of the world!

That is, until a year later, when my world came crashing down. The stresses of adult responsibilities had taken a toll on my premature marriage. My heart was shattered when I walked in on my husband with a lover, and again when I caught him with another woman during an attempt to reconcile a few months later. Then my car was totalled when I was hit by a drunk driver and I ended up having to drop that semester of college to recover from injuries.

This period had a profound impact on how I felt about myself and the decisions I had made throughout my life to this point. While that marriage ended after only 17 months, for the next ten years I agonized over the loss of that love and struggled to understand why things happened as they did. I had loved him so much and was a good and faithful wife. So why did he cheat? Why didn't he choose me in the end? How could he stop loving me when I continued to love him so much? Why wasn't I good enough? These thoughts, coupled with my feelings of profound pain and insecurity, led me to choose other relationships for the wrong reasons and, ultimately, continue the cycle of suffering.

Looking back, what made it such an important part of your life journey?

For me, learning the lessons of love has been an ongoing process, and one that I have yet to master. After my first marriage, I was determined to not make the same mistakes and so I jumped into another relationship with someone that I considered to be the complete opposite. When that didn't work, I hastily followed my longing for love into another marriage to someone I barely knew yet seemed to be the opposite of the guy before. This pattern continued throughout three marriages and several other failed relationships.

With each relationship, my desire to be loved and accepted resulted in me giving up more and more of myself. The ironic part is that my actions were counterproductive. The more I gave of myself, the less pleased my partners were. Each time, I would end up feeling more empty, alone and afraid.

These experiences have taught me a lot about myself. I have identified how, instead of being honest with myself, I tend to try and avoid pain and run from myself. While doing this offers temporary relief, in the long run the results are ultimately more harmful.

My failures have shaped me and blessed me with an enormous amount of strength. I have learned to become self-sufficient and have gained a great deal of confidence, both which have helped me grow my business. This strength allows me to be vulnerable and has sustained me through heartbreak in a way that honours myself and others in the process.

I am also learning to really love myself. I have become much more focused and intentional about what I want. I have learned how to express my needs in a clear and healthy way and have become much better at setting boundaries.

Based on the wealth of knowledge, wisdom and experience that you have now, what would you have liked to say to yourself back then?

Dear Leeanne,

You are an amazing, smart, beautiful and talented girl. The world is a buffet for your choosing. Look at all of the delicious and tantalizing options in front of you, then take your time and consider them wisely before making your selections. While there are no wrong choices, choose consciously and deliberately. Be powerful in your choices, they will shape your life.

You have such a precious heart, sweet girl, and such a capacity for love. You love deeply with all of your body and soul, and your commitment is solid. This is a wonderful quality to possess. Choose those who you bestow this love upon with careful consideration and be sure that they are worthy of this gift before you give it. There is no rush. Give that love to yourself first, that way your heart is always full.

You are good enough, in every way. You can literally do anything you want and have anything you want. You have every opportunity. TAKE THEM! Explore the world. Try new things. Meet lots of people. There is no reason to be afraid.

You are so beautiful. You will have all kinds of relationship partners to choose from. Be picky, picky, picky!!! I know attention feels good; however, that attention will quickly start feeling bad if it's from the wrong guy. You don't owe any guy anything. Make sure you are clear on what you want. Very clear. Then you will know once you find it. When you do find it, take enough time to be sure you are really getting what you think you are getting. Remember, if you marry him, you will have to live with him and deal with him. When you do find him, cherish him.

You have enormous strength. You CAN and WILL get through the hard times. No matter what choices you make, you will experience failures. Embrace them and learn from them. Then pick yourself up and make it happen. Pain may seem scary, but it's a great teacher. It's only by going through the pain and coming out the other side that you will benefit from its lessons.

" You have enormous strength. You CAN and WILL get through the hard times. No matter what choices you make, you will experience failures. Embrace them and learn from them. Then pick yourself up and make it happen "

-Leeanne Lowe-

Resisting and attempting to avoid the pain only serves to amplify and perpetuate it.

Nurture your friendships. No matter how deep you get into a romantic relationship, always maintain friendships with good girlfriends. Guys will break your heart, and you need your girlfriends to be there to help you collect the pieces. Select girlfriends who are like-minded, love you unconditionally and will be honest with you. Be there for them when they need you, too.

Take time to nurture your body and spirit. Invest in your appearance - if you look good you will feel good. Focus on gratitude and abundance. You are so very blessed and many, many good things are coming your way. Expect them and appreciate them.

Above all, be true to yourself. If something doesn't feel right, pay attention. Trust your gut. Make decisions based on what is honest and feels good. Decisions based on guilt and fear will only produce more guilt and fear. Some decisions are complicated and not easy to make. In those situations, take your time and make sure you are clear before proceeding.

Remember, this life is a gift. Make the most of it! There is good everywhere, look for it. Love, laugh and be grateful.

With all my love,

Leeanne

What golden nuggets did you learn from this experience?

There is no reason to rush love or life. It's a paradox - jumping in too fast and trying to force an outcome only serves to delay ultimate gratification. While delaying gratification may seem difficult in the moment, in the end it provides lasting fulfilment.

Be selfish when it comes to your life. It's YOUR life. You need to be true to your own purpose and make choices based on what is authentic and right for you. Giving up yourself to please others results in no one being happy.

What would you tell other women who might be experiencing this in their lives?

Love yourself. Become your own best friend. Follow your bliss and enjoy every moment.

You get to create your own life, so be intentional and selective on the people and experiences you include in it.

What are some of the things you would have changed about that situation if you could have?

I would have slowed things down and waited to get married until after college. I would have created a picture of what I wanted my life to look like, then taken the time to make sure my choice of partner was aligned with my vision.

I would have applied to other schools and explored other educational opportunities.

How can people get in touch with you and see the work you do?

www.empiread.com

You ARE Powerful - Don't Give Up, the Universe Has Your Back

Yvette Taylor, founder of EAM Freedom Limited.

What are you passionate about and how you are contributing to the world?

I work as a transformational mentor and coach, and the creator of EAM – The Energy Alignment Method®. We're on a mission to touch the lives of millions of people using EAM, to enable them to let go of resistant energy, thoughts and emotions.

It is our belief that everyone, can change their life. It doesn't matter who you are, where you're from or what has happened in your life. You CAN change it. Your life can be easy. You can experience more love, more freedom, and more happiness every day. It just takes a shift in your energy and we want to show you how.

Describe a pivotal time in your life.

For me the pivotal time was the young age of 11. It was the turning point between the innocence of childhood and becoming a woman. Although I was far too young I believe it was this point which changed the course of my life.

Based on the wealth of knowledge, wisdom and experience that you have now what would you have liked to say to yourself back then?

My darling Yvette,

I wanted to take this time to write you a letter, to share with you what I now know but didn't when I was young. Right now, you are just eleven years old. Things don't feel great for you; you've got questions, you're angry, you're hurt. It's hard, you're wondering what this life is all about, because it doesn't seem to have been that kind to you. And I get it now. I really do.

For me to explain all the amazing things to come in your life, I need to take you back. Your story begins before you were even born. . . I want you to understand why this had to happen for you to be the person you need to be.

You come from a family of strong, powerful women. Who each have an astounding ability to get back on their feet, no matter how many times they get knocked down. This pattern went back through the generations.

Let's begin with your mum's mum. Your nana was from a wealthy family in a village called Gayle, near Ocho Rios, Jamaica. Her mum had been a sister at the hospital and provided well for your family. Your grandad had left Jamaica and come to the UK to create a better life. Over the years they had grown apart and separated. This meant your mum and her sister were ferried between the two sides of the family, who lived at different ends of the country.

Extended family members were battling to take care of the girls, because with them came the money that your grandad was sending home. At the time, mum had not seen her own mother for years because they wouldn't let them be together. Being so young all she knew was a feeling of loss, heartache and abandonment. She never knew the real love of a father figure in her early years.

Just because they had the money it didn't mean that they took care of the girls. Throughout your mum's childhood, she was not well loved by that family. They were cruel. They were evil. They were violent.

One day, at the age of just seven, your mum was beaten and left for dead in the ditch. Why? Because her uncle said she didn't come in on time for dinner from playing in the bush. Luckily, she was found and rescued.

As she lay in bed recovering from her life-threatening injuries, she remembers waking one morning to hear the early morning bus trundle into the village and toot its horn. Off the bus came the voice of a powerful woman. She knocked on the door to the house and demanded to see the girls. After much arguing and shouting at her uncle, the voice went away.

An hour later she was back, this time with the local police sergeant who demanded that she be allowed to enter the house. As your mum lay in the bed with just her eyes able to turn to the opening door, a smile spread across her face. It was her mum. On hearing what had happened to her little girl, she was here to take them back. NO ONE was messing with her daughters. She strode in and took both your mum and her sister home to safety.

From that day, she spent some loving, happy years living with her mum, her sister and her stepfather. He was a good man too. He was kind and loving. They enjoyed the schooling, the fun, the hugs and support. For a time, life was good.

When your mum was about the same age as you are now, your nana was in hospital. Members of the other family caught news of this and your grandad sent his family to take your mum and her sister to England. Can you imagine the pain in mum's heart as the tears rolled down her face? Watching the only island, she had ever known, and her mum, disappear over the horizon. Not saying goodbye, never knowing if she would return home.

For your mum nothing could replace this great big gaping loss. I wish I could say life got easier for her when she was here. In many ways it was. Your Grandad was a good man, whilst he wasn't loving, he wanted the best for the family.

Your mum never really knew the love of a man who adored her, not in the way she should. Every man she attracted hadn't been kind. Every time she caught sight of real love she would see it whisked away by the overbearing nature of another man in her life.

As she grew up, your mum had four children, two boys and two girls. Those two girls were you and your sister. Sadly, the pattern continued. Your dad was another cruel and unloving man to your mum and to both of you. You know that he works long hours, earns good money and keeps all the money for himself. Every week he gives your mum less than £20 for the family food shopping.

" It is our belief that everyone, can change their life. It doesn't matter who you are, where you're from or what has happened in your life. You CAN change it. Your life can be easy. You can experience more love, more freedom, and more happiness every day. "

-Yvette Taylor-

Which is why she needs to take you on the bus to get the food shopping while your dad nips off to the pub. He won't let her take the car, so he can drive home drunk, again.

Your mum does what she can to take care of you. She loves you more than you know. She is working as a dinner lady and cleaner at the school to make ends meet. To pay for the food you need and your clothes for school.

I hope you one day you understand this is why your 'play time' is spent wandering the empty corridors of the school, finding a teacher to talk to. Or helping your mum to scrub the floors and toilets before you go home. At times I know you sneak out to a friend's house in the village to find some company and play with your friends.

I know you don't understand this right now. You hate the fact she is never there. You hate that your friends have people round for tea and you don't. You hate that no one is at home for you after school. I get it, Yvette, I really do.

Even going home for you does not feel any better. It is not fair that you live your lives on tenterhooks. You shouldn't have to spend your days wondering, "Will it be quiet tonight? Has dad been drinking again? Has he got into another fight at work? Is he going to explode in another fit of rage?" For you and your sister, a good day is one when you've kept quiet, played in your room and stayed out of the way. There have been too many bad days.

I know and remember the pain you feel when the two of you are cowering behind your bedroom door. Or when you're staying silent, hiding in the darkness of the wardrobe, your finger tips are white holding tight to the inside of the door. You feel the tears rolling down your face again as you listen as your mum screams. You hear things breaking as he lays into her for the countless time. Knowing you have left her on the outside trying to protect you, because you didn't eat all your dinner.

Yvette, in a way you are lucky. Being the youngest, your older sister is there to take care of you. She does her best to protect you, she took the brunt of it. At times leaving you both trampled under smashed doors, with black eyes, thumps in the ribs and bruises on your body. Every time, the police would come and go saying it was a "family matter" or "nothing they could do" leaving you waiting for the next time.

I know how many times you have laid there planning how easy it would be to get rid of him. Dreaming about smothering his face with a pillow, stabbing him in the back, hitting him with a saucepan or burying him in the garden, just so this would all stop, and you could feel safe.

You wonder about your friends lives and think, "Do their dads do the same to them?" You sit and watch their dad play at their birthday parties. You watch them smiling as they drive off on another family holiday or day trip out. All the time your heart is breaking wondering why your life just isn't the same. Why can't you be loved and feel normal like your friends.

Well listen to me now... You do not need to be normal, Yvette. You are perfect, you are wonderful, and you are beautiful. There is nothing wrong with you. You don't have to fix it all. You did nothing wrong. You don't have to keep the peace. It is not your fault.

You have been so brave for the last three years, since you were just eight years old you've been fighting. Quite literally for your life. You've missed weeks and months of school. You've missed out on friendships, with other children thinking you were "weird" as you bounced from hospital to home to hospital to home.

I remember so well the look of despair on your mum's face as the doctors kept turning her away, sending you home saying the weight you had put on was just puppy fat. Your mum knew better. Your body had swollen so much you could barely open your eyes. She finally got you in to see the old family doctor who took one look at you and called the ambulance.

Your mum was right; you see, she knew. Your body had shut down. It was not puppy fat but urine which had made you swell up. Your kidneys were near to failure, you were less than 24 hours away from dying. You had developed a rare kidney condition known as nephrotic syndrome. This allowed urine back into your blood which was quickly killing your body, making it shut down.

I know how scared you were being left in a crazy place like hospital on your own. No mum or sister there with you. I remember seeing you standing in the corridor in your nightie, your bare feet on the hospital floor, crying for your mum. She wanted to be there, but she couldn't get there your dad wouldn't bring her in. I know how lost and alone you felt, and it was then you decided that you couldn't rely on anyone.

I am writing to you now because I wanted you to know that it's going to get worse before it gets better. Just know that it DOES get better. I wish I could tell you something different, but I want to prepare you for what is ahead.

I know you are still battling with being ill. The doctors are honestly baffled why they can't keep it at bay. You're going to have to see a specialist and he is going to tell your mum some bad news. The only way they believe they can make you better is a cancer treatment, and that is the last resort before they put you on dialysis for life.

That's going to mean some pretty horrible side effects. Things you're not going to like as little girl. You're going to lose your hair; it will get thin and patchy. You'll never have thick, curly hair again like your sister. You'll judge yourself and the way you look. You'll think all your friends are prettier than you as you look at your podgy face in the mirror. The doctor will tell you that the side effects of this treatment means you can't have children. That is going to be a really hard thing to hear. While it may not bother you too much yet, as you get older the pain will grow.

Now here comes the kicker. You see, you're a strong-minded girl, Yvette. Even at eleven years old you are so much older than your years. You've been through a lot in your young life already. You think you are older when really, you're still a young girl.

You are about to set yourself on a journey where you'll be looking for love in all the wrong places. You crave love, attention and affection. You'll take it from just about anywhere, because it's something you've never felt you had.

Most Saturday nights you'll tell your mum you are staying at a friend's house for a sleep over. Which is true. Except you don't tell her that your friend's dad had gone away and her sister is having her 16th birthday party. Or that you're hanging out drinking and smoking with all her friends, one of which will take a fancy to you. You don't know any better, you'll just love the attention.

While you have kissed boys before and you know 'something' is supposed to happen, you won't expect what comes next.

You'll lie squashed on the bathroom floor; the room is spinning from the vodka. You're in pain as you feel blood spilling all over the bathroom carpet and your innocence disappears.

You'll tell your friend. The sad thing is, she won't believe you. You'll tell her sister and she won't believe you either. You'll get up the next morning and stuff tissue in your knickers as you walk home. You won't dare to tell your mum in case she says something in front of your dad. And you don't want world war three to kick off, so you'll stay quiet.

Just six weeks after that you go to Jamaica for the first time to see your family, back to the place where this pattern of pain began in our family. The irony is not lost on me that you arrive there at the same age our mum left so many years before. This was the first time that you'd see your heritage, the scenery, the culture, and understand the people.

You'll make friends with your cousin who is three years older than you and lives downstairs from your nana's house. You become the best of friends. She takes you down to play at the river, you climb trees and explore in the jungle. One day, on the way back up to nana's house, you stop at run-down shack because she wants to see her "friend".

As she disappears off into the bedroom and you hear the door shut, her friend's friend moves over to you on the sofa. He will start to kiss you and despite you pushing him away, he is five years older and much stronger. Moments later you find yourself half-naked in the cold, hard bathtub. All you can do is lie still, wait for it to be over, and keep your eye firmly watching the knife he is holding as he grips the edge of the bath.

And yet still, you'll think you're strong. You won't say a word. You won't want to get your cousin in trouble. She shouldn't have been at that guy's house and you think to yourself, "Well then neither should I." So again, you keep it to yourself.

Back home again in England a few months on, you'll have this deep, sad pain inside your heart. You'll be angry and lash out and you'll have no idea why. You'll shout, you'll scream, you'll kick, you'll punch, you'll fight.

And then along comes number three. Your babysitter's big brother. You've known him all your life. He invites you round to roll a joint in his bedroom. He is the local dealer, everyone knew him. Every guy wanted to be him, and every girl wanted to be his girlfriend because he has an awesome car. You swoon at the sight of him and, yes, it is another man, filling the gap and giving you attention, you have craved for so long.

Now this one you have to take some responsibility for. You don't exactly fight him off because you'll believe this is just the way things are. You lie once again like a limp dog on his bed watching the spliff burn away in the ashtray before he drives you home.

Again, you'll keep your silence. You're going to keep this pain bottled up for years. You're going to see yourself as an unworthy 'object' that men can do that to. Your mum will freak out as you fall in love with a man eight years older than you when you're just 14 because you think you "love him". To dull the pain, you'll discover drink, drugs and partying. You'll believe that being off your face is better than feeling the darkness of a lost childhood. And for many years this journey will hurt.

Just know that relief isn't too far away. At the age of 17, you discover something powerful. It's called Energy. You learn that you can change how you think and what you feel. It will take time to get to grips with it all. You'll go on an epic adventure trying every single methodology, reading every book and training in every therapy you can to take away this pain. You do your time.

So why did I begin this letter with our mum?

Because these things that are happening aren't just about you and so much of this is not your fault at all.

What I now know and understand is that these patterns are also passed down through the generations. From both sides of the family. Whether you call it DNA or family genetics, I believe (in fact, I know) that it is ALL just energy.

Even though you weren't born, everything that happened to your mum and her mum, and her mum before her, is imprinted in you. I know in our family there are patterns of loss, pain, violence, sexual abuse and abandonment. You came into this life carrying ALL the history of our family's past. It was your soul's journey to break those patterns for everyone past, present and future.

I know now that your dad not being the man you wanted him to be sent you off in search of anyone who would give you attention. Despite it all he didn't know better. He did the best he could with what he knew. I know that on a soul level you all agreed to play this story out together, so that you could experience it all. I know he regrets the life and families that he lost, and that is his life lesson to learn. I know that you love him no matter what because at the end of the day he is still your dad.

Your body getting sick was its way of protecting you, to get you out of the situation. This wasn't just a physical health condition. Your body is amazing. All those years of living at home had taken its toll. This may not make sense to you now, but in Chinese philosophy your kidneys are the seat of fear. While it made you so ill, it also saved you from the fear filled environment you didn't want to be in. Spending so much time in hospital relapsing every time you went home was a response which actually kept you safe.

If you feel like something is wrong, for God's sake don't ever, ever, ever stay quiet again. What happened to you was not your fault. It was not okay. You were young and you didn't know any better, now that doesn't mean you can put the blame on others. In the bigger perspective of life, they had their own stuff too. If you had said something about it, people would have been able to support you. You did NOT have to suffer alone.

Above all else, remember that your mum and your sister love you more than you know and would do anything to protect you. Over the years you gave them so much stress, strain and struggle, and while you fought, all they wanted was to support you, you just couldn't see it.

Please know not all men are like your dad. There are kind and gentle men in your life too. You'll mess some relationships up on the way, but you DO find a man who loves and adores you. His name is Ade and he stands by you no matter what. He will be everything you always wished for when you were young. He is loving and kind. He is amazing and funny. He is thoughtful and caring. He will always do the best by you, and he will be the amazing dad you always wanted for your children.

I also know that the doctors can get it wrong, because in 2014 you will become the luckiest mum in the world giving birth to your beautiful son, Kye. Not everyone gets it right all the time and it IS possible to achieve your hopes and dreams against all odds.

I know that you had to experience all this to become the woman you are today.

If you hadn't none of what you created would have happened.

If you hadn't had this pain, you would have never started your journey of self-discovery to change your life.

If you hadn't chosen this lesson before you arrived in this life you wouldn't have had it.

This is your journey because you ARE strong enough, Yvette.

You ARE amazing.

You ARE powerful.

You ARE beautiful.

You always have been, and you always will be.

Even though you are just eleven years old, I am everything I am because of who you are today. It was you, Yvette, who made me strong.
I want to thank you for the courage, the strength and the determination you showed, even in the face of your greatest fears.

I want to thank you for never giving up, even when life felt so hard and you felt like no one was there to support you.

I want to thank you for the love you still showed to others even when you felt like you were dying inside.

You taught me to stay strong and to find friendship.

You taught me to be kind and to love others.

You taught me to forgive and to let go.

You taught me to keep on going until you find happiness.

These are the lessons I learnt from you; all of these from the life of a young little girl who stood the test of it all so that I could be the woman I am today.

You have no idea how happy your life will be.

You have no idea how many people's lives are changed because of you.

You have no idea how exciting your journey ahead will be.

I never dreamed that I would grow up to be a transformational coach, mentor or guide. After all, what did I have to share? It was something I never could have imagined before (and even have to pinch myself now).
It seems like someone else's life when I think back to where you are to where I am now. Together we are touching the lives of thousands of men and women around the world. Teaching them how to live a life of more happiness, more love and more freedom.

Yvette, I am so proud of you and of everything you've become. All because one amazing little girl wouldn't give up. Whilst at times it may have felt a million miles away, the universe was always there supporting you. It never went away. You just had to ask and listen to hear the message it was sending you.

How did this event change your life?

I don't know how it changed my life because I don't know what the alternative life would have been. I only know what I know now. We only have this one experience and it is up to us to make the best of what we have.

I believe that if I had not had those experiences I would never have ended up here doing what I do today. I would never have had a need to feel better than I did, if everything had been shiny and perfect. I probably would have followed my career to be a lawyer, lived a mediocre life, working nine to five.

I may have been happy. Yet I don't believe it would have given me the sense of love for a life with purpose that I have now.

What golden nuggets did you learn from this experience?

Your body is powerful and will always do its best take care of you.

No matter what happens you can be happy and love life again.

You haven't done anything wrong to deserve this. You are not being punished.

Everyone is doing the best they can with what they think, feel and believe. Never give up on changing your life. This isn't it.

The Universe, God, Jesus, Angels, Allah, Buddha whoever you listen to or whatever name you give it. They are always there.

What would you tell other women who might be experiencing this in their lives?

To anyone else reading my story. Just know you are not alone.
All of those things that happened to you. They hurt. I know.

They made you exactly the person you are today.

And just look at who you are.

You've found your way here to read the amazing stories in this book.

You've asked for this in some way and you made it happen.

No matter what happens in your life it doesn't mean that that's it.

It doesn't have to be your story until the day you die.

YOU have the power to rewrite your story. That time starts now.

What are some of the things you would have changed about that situation if you could have?

I would have been more respectful to my mum. She was doing the best she could with the life we had. Instead of fighting against her and blaming her I would have been more understanding.

I would have told people what had happened and made sure something was done about it. It wasn't right what happened, and it wasn't my fault. I did nothing wrong and I did not have to live with that secret for so many years.

I would have enjoyed much more of my childhood and been a child for longer. I would have played more, laughed more.

I would have had a loving family, quality time exploring the world, holidays and seeing different places together.

Any final words?

Every day you get up is your chance to start again. I know it sounds like a cliché, but your life is yours. No one else's.
The only thing that ever stands in the way of what you want is your energy, what you think and how you feel.

I know that now. It took me a long time to really live it, but now I do. I can't tell you how magic it feels, how far away it feels from the life I had before.
I don't need drink or drugs to feel like that. I don't need love or admiration from anyone except me, and I don't need to expect anything from anyone. Everyone else is off the hook because it is up to ME to make my life happy.
It's the same for you too. If you want to change your life, then change it!
It all begins with changing your energy, thoughts and emotions. When you master doing that, watch your amazing life unfold.

How can people get in touch with you and see the work you do?

If you want to discover more about what I now know, you can find me at www.energyalignmentmethod.com or email us on hello@energyalignmentmethod.com.

Explore how you can change your life by simply shifting energy, thoughts and emotions. Discover the stories and case studies of thousands of people who are doing exactly the same –using EAM, The Energy Alignment Method ®, for themselves too.

The Light Within

Sylvia Baldock, founder and MD of Sylvia Baldock Ltd., unlocking the hidden potential in individuals and teams through powerful profiling, workshops, coaching, writing and inspirational talks.

What are you passionate about and how you are contributing to the world?

My life's work is all about enabling people to connect with who they truly are at their core, to realise the unique value they have to offer the world and to have the confidence and inner belief to step up and let it shine!

Describe a pivotal time in your life that you would like to share.

Let me take you back to a time in my life where I was feeling that life was very restricting and I had a need to break free and find my own pathway.
I was feeling very different from my friends and I was being left out of many of their social activities.

I was fourteen, the hormones were raging, and I had a deep need to feel one of the cool crowd. My strict Baptist upbringing meant I wasn't allowed to experiment with all the normal teenage activities that my school friends were getting so excited about; cinema, discos, make-up, mini-skirts, etc. I couldn't share in their Monday tales of exciting weekends, boys they had kissed, parties they had been to, and I began to feel very left out and as if I just didn't have a voice. Gradually they stopped inviting me and as their friendships deepened over their shared experiences, so I became more and more isolated.

Eventually I rebelled, and after weeks of negotiation with my parents, I gained very grudging permission to go to my first disco. Two more visits to said disco followed and just before my 15th birthday, I met the man who was going to change my life forever.

He was tall, handsome, charismatic, and oh so worldly-wise to a sweet Christian girl!

He swept me off my feet and over the next four intense years he had a huge influence on my personal development and mind-set. I married him at the tender age of 19 and then very quickly realised I had married a chauvinistic bully – not a physical bully, an emotional one!

His raison d'être was to keep me small.

I had to be the 'perfect' little wife, with the immaculate home, producing the best dinner parties, agreeing with his points of view and definitely not looking or smiling at another man or even talking to our male friends for more than the cursory polite exchanges.

I initially fought against this personality 'straight jacket' he was trying to force me into, but after a couple of years of suffering through days, sometimes weeks, of the total silent treatment, I realised that it was easier to play 'small', to conform to his idea of the 'ideal wife'. It was much less painful to shrink into the box he wanted to keep me in than it was to put my head above the parapet and let my true character shine.

I remember dreading hearing his key in the lock, knowing he would be cold and silent, ignoring my questions about what I had done this time to invoke such fury (I frequently didn't have a clue as to why I was being punished).
At other times his mood would suddenly darken when we were out with friends and I would know that I would be subjected to a tirade of abuse when we got home. He told me I had nothing to offer in conversation, that our friends were only friends because of his wit and repartee, and that I had no personality.

I often went to bed early, feeling wretched, dreading the next day and wondering how I was going to survive the year ahead of mental and spiritual torture. I developed eating disorders, fluctuating between bingeing and fasting as he wanted me to be as thin as a supermodel.

I did sometimes get the courage to leave, to go and live with my wonderful mum who would embrace me and shower me with the love and affection that I so craved. She would buy me clothes because I was kept on a strict budget with a very limited wardrobe. He didn't want me to stand out, so my flair for fashion and colour was stifled.

She lived very close to us, so it was way too easy for him to pitch up and turn on the charm. He would always swear to change and persuade me that we were meant to be together. I was dragged back into the web of cruelty and deceit and became increasingly unhappy and then seriously ill with hepatitis, glandular fever and IBS, which are frequently exacerbated by long-term stress. I was then very thin, so that pleased him!

I knew I was living a 'half-life' being a shadow of the woman I was born to be and I felt ashamed of my weakness. He had such a powerful hold over me that I felt paralysed to make a move and go it alone.

I vowed that when I eventually did get away from him, I wanted to help people like me who wanted to break free from their unfulfilling life but felt trapped and disempowered. I wanted to help other people to connect with their true value, to recognise and celebrate their uniqueness and to realise much more of their true potential.

I did eventually break free when he had an affair with one of our 'friends' and suggested that the three of us should live together – what planet was he on?!

As I look back on those unhappy years now, I barely recognise that young, vulnerable girl who just longed to be loved and to be accepted as part of the crowd.

I know that I was meant to go through that pain and learn all the lessons that challenging time taught me, so I could fully understand the anguish of living life as a shadow of the person you were born to be.

It's hard to describe, but it's a bit like being desperate to share the most exciting news with the people you love and suddenly being struck dumb. It's like having the most amazing story to tell but never being allowed to use your voice. It becomes this pent-up energy inside you, which eats away at your confidence and self-esteem and leaves you feeling nauseous, empty, and helpless.

Looking back, what made it such an important part of your life journey?

Those years of mental torture have given me the foundation for everything I do in my work today.

I fully understand the pain of living life in the shadows of a bully, whether that is a life partner or a work colleague or boss.

I can see now that it was his upbringing with a dominant, chauvinistic father that shaped his map of the world and his attitude towards women. His insecurities made him want to dominate me and make me feel as insecure as possible and totally dependent on him. He needed to feel he was in control and that I couldn't survive without him.

I also understand how easy it is to shrink into the shadows, to feel you have nothing to offer to others and that you have nothing relevant to say. You feel powerless and too insecure to stand out from the crowd like this poignant quote:

"Shrinking in a corner, pressed into the wall; do they know I'm present, am I here at all?" - Lang Leav, Love & Misadventure.

The greatest lesson of all is that no matter how much someone tries to suppress your spirit, no matter how much they try to stamp out your personality, and no matter how much they erode your self-esteem, there is a shining light inside you that they are powerless to destroy. It may have become clouded in those shrouds of self-doubt and low self-esteem. It may have built up many layers of limiting self-beliefs over the years and it may have become as imperceptible as a barely flickering candle, but no-one can snuff out that light. It is always there, lurking in the shadows just waiting for someone to stir the embers, to re-ignite the flame and to bring our inherent warmth and wisdom to the world again.

I learned that I have great inner resilience and that no matter what life throws at me, I will find the strength not only to deal with it, but also to learn from it and to come out stronger and wiser with life lessons to share with my community.

" Wherever you are, be totally 'present'. You cannot change one iota of something that happened a second ago never mind an hour/week/month/year ago. So, why dwell on it? It is destructive; it lowers your energy and diminishes your 'presence'. "

-Sylvia Baldock-

I so resonate with the wonderful words of Nick Williams:

"When you walk through your fear, you become inoculated against it, on the other side of your fear is a whole new sense of freedom."

I now make sure I am scared regularly and encourage my clients to do the same. I believe we should always be stepping out of our comfort zone and into our 'stretch' zone. That stretch zone then quickly becomes our 'comfort zone' and then we stretch into our 'discomfort zone' and so on.

We were meant to be continually evolving and developing our skills and it is so exciting when you have done something scary and come through with flying colours – it is such an adrenalin rush!

One of my favourite mantras is 'I am powerful beyond measure' and I truly believe we all have such a deep well of potential that we are only ever scratching the surface of.

Based on the wealth of knowledge, wisdom and experience that you have now what would you have liked to say to yourself back then?

My Darling Girl,

I feel your pain so acutely. I know how desperately unhappy and worthless you feel right now and I know you feel you have failed.

I watched you cry yourself to sleep last night, wondering what on earth you have done to deserve this unhappy and unfulfilling life.

I know you were yearning to be that happy little girl again, playing in the sunshine with your friends and big brothers, not a care in the world. You longed for that life of fun and love and laughter. You remembered how much you loved others to have fun, how you made them laugh with your antics and your mimicry.

That all seems like another life away. You feel such a sense of loss of yourself, you feel you no longer know who you are, what you want and what you have to offer others, if anything at all!

You are criticised at every turn, belittled, made to feel small and insignificant, and you feel it is all your fault.

Let me tell you, dear girl, you are not to blame for your unhappiness. You have married a man who is desperately insecure. He grew up with a controlling, alcoholic father who ruled the roost with a rod of iron and that was his role model.

He actually feels desperately insecure. He knows he is not as bright as you. He went to a less academic school, achieved far fewer qualifications and was brought up in a less affluent area which has made him feel inferior. The only way he knows how to deal with that is to control you. To make you feel small and insignificant so he feels more important.

He loves himself far more than he loves you and will do everything he can to boost his own self-esteem whilst eroding yours.

He knows you have a strong inner core and that you would be so much better off without him, so he keeps making you feel inadequate. He is terrified you will leave him so he controls everything, so you feel dependent on him, that's why he keeps telling you that you couldn't survive without him.

His insecurity feeds his pathological jealousy, which feeds his cruel words to make you feel unattractive and undesirable.

I know you long to indulge your love of colour and style and feel stifled in the same clothes you have to wear over and over again. It's just another way in which he can keep you feeling small and insignificant.

I also know you were brought up to believe that marriage is for life - that old saying: 'You made your bed now lie in it' keeps ringing in your ears!

My darling, please believe me when I say, 'this too will pass'. This is a really challenging phase of your life that you are passing through and the lessons you are learning right now will transform the lives of thousands of people in the years to come.

Let me tell you, Sylvia, that there is a time coming in your future when all of this will make sense. The pain and suffering you are experiencing will give you such deep insight into the feelings of the people you will coach and train when you are older.

You will create transformational workshops and talks that will literally change peoples' lives.

Sylvia, believe me when I tell you that you have so much joy and abundance ahead of you.

You will find the strength to move on from this unhappy marriage when the time is right. It will be painful and tough for a while, but you will come out of your shell like a caterpillar in a chrysalis that transforms into a beautiful butterfly, ready to spread your wings and fly.

You will meet a man who loves you unconditionally and have two wonderful daughters who will bring you the family love and joy you so crave. Your bond will be so strong that you will share many magic times together, secure in the knowledge that you are always there for each other, and family always comes first.

This is the rock on which you will build your business, knowing you are loved deeply and supported unconditionally.

Inside of you is an incredible light, which is your unique 'presence'. Right now, it is shrouded in layers of negative messages, criticism, and limiting self-beliefs, nurtured by his need to keep you small, but believe me when I say no-one can extinguish your light, and one day you will shine so brightly that people will be drawn to you like moths to a flame. They will want to know how you sparkle with such fervour and you will enable them to connect with who they truly are at their core and to stand up and let their own uniqueness shine!

With my deepest love.

Your older self. Xxx

What golden nuggets did you learn from this experience?

I learned that life is too short to be bitter, resentful, angry. Harbouring and nurturing those feelings only hurts me and diminishes my power and my presence.

I long ago learned to let go of those feelings and instead learned to feel pity for a man who lived such an insecure and fearful life.

It has taught me to let go of negative feelings quickly and feel compassion, empathy and understanding.

I know that whatever life throws at me, I can find the strength within me to not only get through the difficult times, but to learn from them and to feel empowered by them.

What would you tell other women who might be experiencing this in their lives?

Take time out for you. Do everything you can to feel strong physically, mentally and spiritually. Eat and sleep well, get out in the fresh air, commune with nature and appreciate the beauty all around you. Exercise regularly to keep fit and release those feel-good endorphins, which will help to get you through those tough days.

Take time to meditate and just 'be' in the moment and wherever you are be totally 'present' rather than dwelling on the problems you have at home.
Spend time regularly with people who love you and people who inspire you - they will lift you up and help you to realise more of your true value.
Try to understand why your partner is the way he or she is. Look at their background, their upbringing, their relationships, and be assured that their behaviour is rooted in their past rather than it being your fault.

What are some of the things you would have changed about that situation if you could have?

I would have stood up for myself more.
I would have developed more interests and hobbies outside the marriage to

bring more independence and fulfilment to my life.
I would have sought help instead of trying to cope on my own and pretend that everything was OK.

Any final words?

Wherever you are, be totally 'present'. You cannot change one iota of something that happened a second ago never mind an hour/week/month/year ago. So, why dwell on it? It is destructive; it lowers your energy and diminishes your 'presence'.

Equally, none of us know if we are going to be here tomorrow, so stop waiting for that perfect time in the future when you are your ideal weight, have the ideal partner, the dream job or home, financial security – that Utopia may never come.

The only thing we can be 100% sure of and impact on right now, is the present. So, wherever you are, live in the moment. Give the people you are with the gift of 'undiluted listening', focusing totally on them and not what's going on in your life.

When you are totally present, life becomes so much easier. We take time to appreciate the sunshine, the bird song, the changing seasons, children's laughter, and life becomes a daily joy of discovery of the universe, yourself, and others.

When you are going through those tough and challenging times, always remember no-one can extinguish your inner light and it will shine brightly once again – remember 'this too will pass'.

How can people get in touch with you and see the work you do?

http://www.sylviabaldock.com/   http://www.inspirationalspeaker.uk
sylvia@sylviabaldock.com   https://www.linkedin.com/in/sylviabaldock
http://www.facebook.com/sylvia.baldock
http://twitter.com/Sylviabaldock
http://www.youtube.com/user/sylviabaldock

It's Okay to Be Me

Laura Ceppelli, founder and creator of 'Heartcorebody'

What are you passionate about and how you are contributing to the world?

It is my mission for women to experience a practice that works deep into the heart, core and body, empowering them to be the best they can be, connecting themselves to universal energy, so they can get on with their awesome lives as supported, and as smoothly as possible.

I believe that looking after ourselves this way improves the way we feel about ourselves, how we communicate in our relationships, and thus giving more meaning and quality to how we experience our lives. When a woman feels fit, healthy, connected and balanced this ripples into the home and into communities.

When a woman shines her light, the whole world becomes a brighter place. We are all enough, perfect in our imperfection and capable of anything. Accepting ourselves and being ourselves is essential for a happy, healthy life. As I travel through my 40s and beyond, it's my mission to use my skills to help as many women as I can feel great and vital, to know how fabulous they are already. Exactly as they are. That is why I developed a blended practice called Heartcorebody in Barcelona. Heartcorebody combines the principles of Pilates with Kundalini Yoga techniques in a capsule class. It is the total recalibration of body and mind; toning, strengthening, improving posture, uplifting, and energising, as well and nurturing, and connecting us to our inner selves.

Describe a pivotal time in your life that you would like to share:

As a child I innocently told my mum I was "starving" at a moment where she couldn't cope with me using that word. Deeply moved by the 1984 Ethiopian famine pictures that were coming into our home at the time, she was looking at in that moment - seeing children who really were starving. What followed programmed me into feelings of shame, guilt and unworthiness that have lasted a lifetime. Always feeling bad for wanting more, always feeling that to put my needs first was bad, always feeling ashamed to be me. I felt guilty for being alive. On a scale of traumatic childhood experiences, it wouldn't be considered traumatic at all, but my childish interpretation and the repercussions have been real and deep for me.

Looking back what made it such an important part of your life journey?

I was fully bulimic for about 20 years and have been in recovery for the last 8 years. For the first 5 years of recovery I used tools and techniques to control urges, occasionally falling off, but always getting back on the wagon. For the last 3 years I feel as recovered as I could ever be, where I no longer have urges to overeat, binge and purge at all, however, I still have tendencies to control and watch what I eat and keep myself in shape. I'm still working it out. It is not lost on me that I have chosen a career which has a physical focus and requires a lot of movement and exercise. I guess we never fully recover but there is freedom now in my life and I don't feel the same way as I did. My relationship with my body, my connection to who I really am, and my place on the planet are so much healthier and so I don't punish myself any longer this way.

Based on the wealth of knowledge, wisdom and experience that you have now, what would you have liked to say to yourself back then?

My Darling Younger Self,

It was the summer of 1984 and you were eight years old. It was the school holidays and you can remember the sun was shining. Your mum made you an open pâté sandwich on fresh, French baguette (which was pretty special in your 80s Welsh village) and you were in heaven as you devoured it, so soft and delicious. Mmmmmmm... You finished it but still felt you could have eaten more. It was just so nice. What harm could there be in asking for a bit more of the tasty snack? What happened next changed you, the way you saw yourself, and your relationship to your world forever. It was only a moment, a moment so insignificant in the life of your mum that she doesn't even remember it, but for you that moment is eternal.

You returned to the kitchen to ask Mum if you could have a bit more bread and pâté. "Mum, I'm starving," you said innocently, "Can I have some more, please?"

Your mum was at the kitchen table reading the Sunday Times magazine and she looked up. You saw tears streaming down her face as she looked at you, you saw pain in her eyes which you interpreted as scorn. Your mum, already distressed and emotional, was made angry by the word "starving" and directed this at you. Your mum thrust the magazine at you and you saw the images of the emaciated children, dying of thirst and hunger, in rags and covered in flies so, so skinny and ill.

You felt so, so bad. You were only eight years old and you had never seen these types of images before. Immediately you felt what you now know to be guilt and shame rise up through your entire body until you were drowning and totally engulfed in these intense feelings that were so new and so painful. Your mum full of pain herself, screamed at you with such anger and rage, with no idea of the significance of her words on you, "No!! You are not starving!" she said, "Look at these pictures - THESE children are starving, not you!! No, you can't have any more, you have had enough. You are just being greedy. You are spoilt rotten, you kids!" (This is what I remember her saying, but I can't be sure the words are exact).

Firstly, know this, darling 8-year-old Laura. Nothing you did made your mum angry. The pain was inside her and she did not mean to hurt you with this emotional outburst. It was directed at you as you were there in the firing line and she didn't know that this would have such an impact on your self-esteem and development. It was not her fault and she didn't mean it. It's how the human operates, directing internal pain outwardly and, unless you are aware, you cannot usually control it. We all lose it from time to time and can't know the repercussions. The word "starving" in your comfortable well-fed western world home triggered something in your mum, and the feeling of sadness and helplessness for all of the people. Of course, you were only using learned language; it is still a common expression, albeit not very nice, used when one is hungry. You were absolutely not to know its significance and are not responsible for your mother's upset and rage about this. There is no blame and it was the combination of many factors coming together that coded the intense emotions into your subconscious. You are sensitive and seeing the images of the suffering people in Africa made you realise your privileged life for the first time and you felt deep shame and guilt about this. The words of your mother, "You have had enough, no you can't have more, you are just being greedy, you are spoilt", hit hard and have been exaggerated so you felt guilty for everything, and you have felt in the past that you do not deserve even to be alive. This is not real, darling Laura. Not at all.

You took the magazine behind the sofa in the living room and sobbed and sobbed over the pictures. You can't remember what you were thinking, or how long you were there, but what you were doing was etching deeply into your psyche inaccurate, limiting and debilitating beliefs about who you are and how to be in this world. Much more damaging than the words of your mum in the moment, that a less sensitive child might have sulked a little bit about before moving on to the next game, was affirming over and over of how 'terrible' you were, and how 'spoilt', 'greedy' and 'undeserving' you were.

It was the message you told yourself and concentrated on so intently it became true for you. These false beliefs become etched in your heart and subconscious and you have believed that to want and need things is shameful and greedy. You have felt you don't deserve to have more, you mustn't want more of anything, to want more is bad. You have felt you are a bad person for wanting more. You must be ashamed of who you are, always. You don't deserve a nice life when there are people who have nothing. Why should you be alive when people are dying? You must not ask for anything you need or want. What you want, or need does not matter. You are not important enough to have your needs met. You have always felt you must walk with your head down and apologise for who you are. You must be ashamed and apologise for being you. It is not okay to be you.

'It's not okay to be you' is what you have lived with since that day and it has taken you on a journey over the most difficult terrain. But it IS most definitely okay to be you, Laura. More than okay. You triumph by being you. You are strong. You have courage and resilience, and have forged forward creating lovely friendships and relationships, but please do love yourself. Love yourself first, darling Laura, and know your needs and wants are important and essential. Part of your charm is having absolutely no idea of your gifts or what a positive, vibrant energy you have. However, knowing these sooner, knowing that you count, will help you share them with the world and bring you more fulfilment and confidence to live your live to your fullest potential. Having confidence in yourself, showing yourself and your

" You are a beautiful, compassionate soul, and the women of the world need you to step up and be the mirror to show them that the power is inside them too. "

-Laura Ceppelli-

truth will cut out many years of never feeling enough because you were not in tune with believing that you are enough already. Be yourself - always. You are enough - always. Trust yourself and believe in yourself.

Years of working to reprogram the subconscious with new beliefs that serve you and align you with your true universal nature as a human being were worth it. You now know they aren't true, but they were scratched so deep you have spent much of your adult life trying to erase them. Well done, Laura!! It's not easy to get right down to the wound and be in the pain, and build yourself back up piece by piece, unlearning the learned patterns of thinking and behaving.

Your eating disorder may or may not be down to this one event. You are a sensitive human being and there could be many reasons why you became bulimic at the age of 14, but almost certainly low self-esteem and self-worth, feeling 'less than...', experiencing big emotions and being unable to express them freely played a role. New feelings and emotions that were brought up and stuffed back down, feeling guilty and ashamed of expressing yourself and your needs, had serious implications on how you lived and behaved from then on.

My darling Laura, go to a professional expert sooner rather than later so you can do all this unravelling earlier and maybe, with support, an addiction will not develop. Maybe the timing has been perfect just the way it is, as this has been your soul's journey, but I am sad you suffer for over 20 years. I feel your bulimia, if necessary at all, should be a teenage coping mechanism that you outgrow as a young woman and not stay with you well into your 30s.

You can do it and working on healing sooner may save you so much time and pain. The power is inside of you. It always has been. Know that yours (I speak about my own experience and beliefs and do not want to generalise here across all eating disorders and addictions) is a subconscious decision you have made to protect and soothe yourself and deal with your emotions. It becomes an addiction and it is a driven by low self-worth and inability to take responsibility. It's full of fear. I know when you are in the throes of it, it is like you have been possessed and you have no control. It's deep. It's in your subconscious. You are an addict. It is powerful which is why, ignored, it remains in your life for so long. This is why you need real help and support from a professional and to be honest with yourself. This has prevented you from blossoming sooner. This has kept your esteem and self-worth low. This has kept you from believing in yourself and reaching for the stars. It's kept you from being of service to the world.

Ignoring it, pretending you don't have a problem and self-managing takes so much of your energy that you cannot be the person you need to be, shining her light and sharing her gifts. This black and heavy cloak you wear for so long, but disguise as a bright and happy sun dress, is exhausting. The pretending to be fine is exhausting. The time and physical consequences on your life are a huge waste of time. You CAN do it and you DO, do it!! It all works out and you'll be fine and are the person you are today because of your journey so don't beat yourself up. Just get well and be happy. Do not waste this time.

Don't be afraid of anything, Laura. You are stronger than you know. You will find Pilates which strengthens your weak and debilitated body, and gives you focus and relieves your stress. Your mind becomes more balanced and calmer, and your esteem improves as you walk taller with confidence, your muscles toned. As your body becomes lengthened and flexible, your mind expands and becomes more flexible too. You start taking care of your body and making better choices when it comes to food and men. You are open to meeting new people and taking on new challenges which, in turn, broadens your horizons adding the building blocks to real happiness, breaking free from the self-imposed prison of your critical thoughts.

As you change the beliefs about yourself, the urges become fewer and as you become more engaged in life, fall in love and have a baby, life is so full and has more meaning, so the bulimia fades into the background, although does not disappear until a bit later.

It won't be until you resettle in Barcelona and start training to teach Kundalini Yoga that your recovery feels like you are done with it. I can't tell you when or how to flip the switch exactly, but Kundalini Yoga was big in your life and worked for you. You found peace, and your place in the bigger picture. You shine and connect with people and have a gift for empathising and making people feel really comfortable with you. Know your gifts and have confidence to share them with the world. Share your story and help others know they are not alone and that there is hope.

You are a beautiful, compassionate soul, and the women of the world need you to step up and be the mirror to show them that the power is inside them too. You must not be the victim in this but be an empowered woman and support the healing of others. Go forth, young Laura, and be of service to those who need you and your work. As Louise L Hay writes in "You Can Heal Your Life" for the Bulimia Affirmation, you will say it ten thousand times in your healing. "You are loved and nourished and supported by life itself. It's safe for me to be alive." It's true and I love you.

Yours most lovingly,

Laura XX

What golden nuggets did you learn from this experience?

Although part of me knows that this was my journey, the experience that I had to go through, but part of me would want my younger self to avoid it altogether and to not have suffered silently and alone for so long. I can see now, and would like to illuminate to my younger self, and others vulnerable to self-harm, that the eating disorder was slow suicide, and to stay silent and alone increases its hold and intensity. I was totally gripped by this fear of life, fear of love, fear of success and fear of shining. Fear of being a thriving human being. Fear to be alive. Full of shame. I no longer feel this way, I love my life, I'm learning to love myself, and I hope in sharing my story I can be of service and help young women going through this. There is hope.

What would you tell other women who might be experiencing this in their lives?

We all have our stories and for me life is like Soul School and we all have different things to learn along the way. Our journeys teach us what we need to know, to be the best we can be, to inspire and help shine our light and help each other. They are required to grow; however, it does not serve the world if you play at being small and apologise for who you are. You can help more by creating, showing up and adding to the beauty and richness of life.

It's hard when you are in the grips of addiction to see yourself as a worthy, deserving person with freedom and hope in your reach, but you are, and it's possible with support. You have to FEEL it in your body and soul and not just read or hear it. You just need to know, not academically, but KNOW through experience, that you are a child of the universe, just as important as and equal to any other human on the planet. There is always a way. If I can, you can.

What are some of the things you would have changed about that situation if you could have?

If I knew my last purge was going to be my last I would have taken note, but I didn't know. It became less and less and was no more. I didn't need it any more to comfort me. I stopped thinking about it. Food became my friend for the first time, but my emotions became my friend for the first time too. As I felt my body change inside and out, my mind changed, and my spirit finally connected with this world through my work. The fact I could feel my emotions safely and express them safely, was when I finally understood, truly, madly, deeply that I am okay exactly as I am. No more stuffing down, or numbing them, or keeping secrets or pretending. I cry more now but I laugh more too. I love more. I am enough. It's okay to be me. I am able to ask for what I want and need. It serves the people who I love to be authentic and honest about how I feel and what I want. It's better for me and for everyone.

Any final words?

Fortunately, apart from having no enamel left on my very thin teeth, the damage I have wreaked on my body over the years appears not to be permanent. I have been very, very lucky to be able to get myself out of the grips of such mental turmoil and live a happy, kind life. It's been my journey and I feel blessed. I have met amazing people and had the most incredible experiences and I can't regret anything about my life, but if I were to give 8-year-old Laura a message, I would hold her hand through the events on that day and whisper in her ear, "You are enough. It's okay to be you and have wants and needs. It's okay to ask for more. You are not responsible for your mother's upset or the suffering in Africa. It's not your fault. Do not feel ashamed to be you."

I would tell 14-year-old Laura to get help sooner and not to ignore the pain for so long. "You can do it. You can get over this. You can shine your light and make the world a brighter place, just be yourself. You need you to be yourself. Everyone needs you to be yourself."

How can people get in touch with you and see the work you do?

Thank you very much for reading my story. I love that we are all collaborating, sharing, blowing the lid of old taboos, and inspiring and supporting each other. If you are suffering yourself or love someone who is, please reach out to me at info@lauraceppelli.com, or if you would like to know more about me, my story, or my work, contact me, or come over to my website www. lauraceppelli.com. Feel free to join my members list to get videos, updates, and inspiration; loads of value to help you find connection whilst rocking your world.

The Key Element to Accepting Yourself

Rhiannon Griffiths. Acupuncturist, coach, author, yin yoga teacher & creator of The Five Element Life.

What are you passionate about and how you are contributing to the world?

I have been living a 'Five Element Life' for over a decade now; living in sync with nature, the cycles of the seasons, what our bodies and emotions need at differing times of the year to keep balanced and healthy on all levels. I am incredibly passionate about sharing this ancient wisdom from Chinese medicine with people all over the world. But even more crucially life changing for me (and you), is my absolute love affair with understanding The Five Elements, and discovering which Element is our own particular one, i.e. our 'Element Personality Type'.

I hold space for you to re-centre and realign to your truth, reconnect you to yourself, and the true energetic vibration of your authenticity. I seek to empower people (particularly women) globally, by encouraging you to work WITH your body, your emotions, your strengths, your challenges and gifts. None of them are to be ashamed of, or need to be 'fixed'. It is my mission to be part of the current, massively important self-love, self-care, personal development movement that is finally giving permission to women to just be.

My wish for you, and for everyone, is to live fully empowered by the in-depth understanding and acceptance that this brings, to live from the power and strength of your Element, to authentically 'Be in your Element'.

Describe a pivotal time in your life you want to share.

The first week I attended class at The College of Integrated Chinese Medicine and started learning the basics of the Five Elements was a pivotal time in my life. It was as though everything finally fell in to place. The dark clouds parted, and the sunshine came out – clarity and light and meaning arrived. New perspectives on life and health, philosophy and spirituality, and balance and depth, spoke deeply to me, and made such beautiful sense. Suddenly a whole new way of understanding myself was revealed and this was on every level – my feelings, my motivations, my ways of being in the world, my body imbalances and my susceptibility to certain illnesses.

I was also able to understand other people's behaviours, triggers and driving forces. I saw my friends and family from a different perspective. I saw them from the space of their particular Element, and it was such an "Aha!" moment; so enlightening and revealing. Understanding that people's reactions are often nothing to do with you, and everything to do with their Element and the energy around that, brings such freedom. You no longer take things as personally and you can often give them what their Element needs, leading to better relationships.

It was life-changing, like reaching a secret hidden higher level on this video game of life. I could view the world through five-element-tinted-glasses, and I was collecting bonus points and magical stars, seeing things that other 'players' could not see. I felt excited, invigorated and energised!

I was able to (possibly for the first time in my life) have compassion, love and understanding for myself. Finally understanding what it meant to be a Water Element personality type allowed me to breathe; with its beautiful and complex themes of fear and bravery, drive, the need for safety and reassurance, depth and overwhelm, wisdom and sensitivity.

For the first time I had tangible reasons as to why I had struggled with all these themes in my life. For the first time I felt like I was truly seen, as the teacher describing a Water Element person was describing me perfectly. For the first time I had permission to be my true self, warts and all, positives and negatives, gifts and challenges – the full, powerful Water spectrum – without feeling that I had to fix or change the bad bits, even if they were different to everyone else's, or what everyone else thought I should be.

Up until this point I felt like my way of being in the world was wrong, that my emotions weren't valid, that I shouldn't need so much rest, that I shouldn't feel everything so deeply, but now I had a 'why'. Being a Water Element person was the reason WHY I felt certain things – paralysing fear, overwhelming emotion, deep analytical over-thinking, not being able to trust the future. Understanding the Five Elements, and particularly Water, was like the missing piece of the jigsaw, like a key which unlocked everything for me. And other people's Elements provide the reasons as to why THEY feel specific things, different things, different things to me as a Water type, but it reveals the reason for them too. The Five Elements are such a precious gift and I am so grateful that the universe guided me to this ancient wisdom.

Looking back, what made it such an important part of your life journey?

It was such an important part of my life journey because the process of studying to be an acupuncturist was the most incredible journey of self-growth, self-understanding and self-acceptance. It was so much more than gaining another degree and learning point location, anatomy and physiology, or Chinese medicine.

I fondly remember sitting in a café, drinking a green tea and describing this time to my mum, as the moment I could FINALLY blossom and bloom into my true self. And it really felt like it had been a long time coming; it was an awakening, a celebration, and a homecoming. I came home to my reason for being on the planet, but I also came home to myself.

I had struggled with feeling different for so many years, feeling as though I was on the outside of everything, feeling trapped, suffocated and misaligned. I had felt as though I had to do certain things and be a certain way to be accepted, to be successful, to have positive prospects. I felt so much pressure to do well in school and have straight A-grades to get accepted to university, all to get a good nine-to-five job that paid well, which ultimately translated (in my mind) into having a safe and secure future, which is a huge motivating factor for a Water Element type, despite not knowing anything about Water at that time.

It felt totally out of the question to do anything else other than the 'norm' and do really well at it, yet I suffered with depression and anxiety for most of my teenage years. After graduating with a first-class degree at Bournemouth University and starting an advertising career in London, both my emotional and physical health started to suffer. I had tonsillitis every other fortnight and still I continued to do the London commute on the train and the tube, work long hours, and excel at my job. My body was screaming at me, but I persisted with 'what I should be doing' at this stage in my young graduate life rather than what I was MEANT to be doing in the world.

The universe had bigger plans for me and eventually I listened. In floods of tears and feeling utterly paralysed around trying to make the 'right decision', I just announced that I thought I was meant to be an acupuncturist. And I didn't even really know why, it just felt right, like it was meant to be. So many people commented on how brave they considered my quick change of career to be – but to me, it felt natural and normal, nothing to do with bravery (again exhibiting classic Water Element traits, that I was yet to learn about).

I finally listened to my heart, my intuition and my body. My purpose revealed itself, and everything flowed beautifully from there. Being an acupuncturist is just so aligned with the core of my authentic self – it was like having permission to finally embody all of my quirks and magic, having permission to understand life, people and emotions from the deepest level, having permission to live and experience the world differently.

In the past, this was a feeling state, or a way of being that I never thought I would get to. I felt as though feeling happy and aligned and free was something for other people, not for me. Becoming an acupuncturist and learning about the Five Elements was like shining a light onto something that I had felt I needed to keep hidden away for so many years. I stepped into my power, my purpose and my passion. I felt connected to an authentic, higher meaning in my life. To my surprise and delight, I felt fulfilled and happy that these emotions and this way of living was possible for me after all.

Based on the wealth of knowledge, wisdom and experience that you have now what would you have liked to say to yourself back then?

My dearest, darling Rhiannon,

This is a healing letter for you, because I know how hard you are finding life right now in these teenage years, how scared you feel about the future and how overwhelming and terrifying everything feels... it's paralysing, I know, and you cry, you really cry... and you wonder if things will ever feel any better, if you will ever be happy, or if you're even capable of being happy, that perhaps it's only for other people, not you, not us...

"Even if you are different to absolutely everyone else in your life, it's ok.
You do not need fixing. You do not need to be the same as them. You do not need to feel the same feelings that they do. Nor do you need to hide, avoid or squash down your feelings because they are too big or too intense. "

-Rhiannon Griffiths-

I know your emotions are strong and overwhelming, and you feel out of control, unable to cope with the depth and intensity of them. I know how petrifying the meltdowns can be when they sweep you up and take you on a tsunami ride of tears and fears, and everything comes spilling out with force.

I know you feel anxious most of the time, you suffer with nightmares, hate sleeping in the dark and you can't watch scary movies; so however many times the girls at school invite you for sleepovers, you do not go. And that is ok, honestly, although it doesn't feel like it right now, I promise, it IS ok. I know you feel so sad, and so alone, and so different. You feel so incredibly different to everyone else, as though you don't belong and you don't fit in, as though you're not really for this world, that no one understands you, that you're too emotional, too sensitive, too deep, too different, too weird, too much.

I'm writing to tell you to take away the word 'too'. Delete that word now. I'm writing to tell you there is nothing wrong with you. Absolutely nothing. Yes, you ARE emotional and sensitive and deep and different and (a little) weird (ok, beautifully weird, let's reframe this as wonderfully quirky, shall we?), and yes, you MIGHT sometimes be too much for some people but that's ok, they are not your people.

It wasn't until I reached this decade of thirty-something where I felt genuinely ok about dropping the 'too'. I know now that was far too long to worry about what other people think. It was too long to feel bad about being different, it was too long to feel like there was something wrong with me.

I want you to drop the 'too' right now. Please don't waste the next twenty years struggling with the beauty and unique amazingness that is you. Please know that all these things you are currently grappling with and being made to feel bad about — as though your way of being in the world, or the way you feel every single thing so deeply, is 'wrong' or 'not normal' — these, my gorgeous girl, are your biggest GIFTS. These aspects of you are the things that make you who you are, and make you good at what you do, what you are destined to do, what I do now.

And this is because you, my cautious little love, are a gorgeous, wise, deep Water Element person. Ok, here comes the spoiler alert – you become an acupuncturist with an obsession for the Five Elements, yes, honestly, and I know you'll be reading this thinking, "But I am massively needle-phobic!" – and yes, you are, but acupuncture is not as bad or as terrifying as you're thinking it is right now. It will honestly open up something breathtakingly wonderful for you. You will finally be able to blossom and bloom into your true self and this is the most important information I need to share with you right now. Everything finally fell in to place when I understood what it meant to be a Water Element person, and I really wish with every fibre of my being that I had known it earlier.

So, this is why I want to tell you all this now. I want to tell you how knowing your dominant Element is so powerful and empowering. This is what I want for you right now. I want you to know that by understanding that you are a Water Element person, you can understand why you have these characteristics, emotions and behaviours, why you feel different to those around you. I want you to know that being Water is ok, it is more than ok, it is perfect. I want you to know you are Water NOW, because it will help you to finally accept yourself, like yourself, LOVE yourself, and truly have permission to just be your true self. I don't want you to have to wait another ten years to start to know this stuff; I want this for you NOW.

Water has many guises – from the calm, still, peaceful lake with hidden depths underneath, to the giant wave that comes crashing down with power and force. The gentle strength of Water is most obvious when thinking of the small, determined trickle that finds its route out through the hardest of rocks.

When I first found out that I was a Water Element personality type and started to learn exactly what that meant, a whole new level of understanding myself, my emotions and my behaviours was available to me, and I want to share that with you. You ARE super emotional, highly sensitive, incredibly driven and often get called a wise old soul. Your classmates often comment on what a calming, reassuring influence you have. You find that second part hard to understand right now, as you only ever feel scared, cautious and fearful, constantly risk-assessing, constantly in fight-or-flight mode, never feeling fully safe in the world, or safe trusting the future. You wonder how they cannot see this side of things in you; to you it feels big and obvious and life-controlling. You wonder how anyone could ever see you as calm and reassuring. These, my love, are all beautiful characteristics of the Water Element, your Element – some of these Water characteristics or emotions are easier to navigate than others, that is true, but ALL of them make up the amazing, fabulous you.

It is because of Chinese medicine I now know that I am not a freak or a weirdo. There is nothing wrong with me, I do not need fixing. And honestly, darling girl, there is NOTHING wrong with YOU, and YOU don't need fixing. Even though right now you find that hard to believe, I want you to know that now at age 14. Just because you have different emotions or behaviours to others around you, it doesn't mean YOU are the one that is different or wrong, it's just because you are a different Element personality type to them, and that's ok.

I know you are finding it hard to trust all of that, to trust yourself, trust the universe, trust the future, trust that everything is going to work out. But that's just another beautiful aspect of being Water.

Oh, and one last thing. Stick with putting Biology as one of your A-level subjects. Yes, people will try to talk you out of it; they will say it doesn't make sense with your other two choices of Communications and Business Studies. They will tell you that you won't need it to go to Bournemouth University. You get there, by the way. I know your fears around this are so massive – let them go, beautiful girl, it all works out, and living by the sea is perfect for you. But yes, they will tell you that biology won't be needed to study Advertising and Marketing Communications down on the south coast. Don't listen to them; you enjoy Biology, and you're good at it. The universe does know what it is doing, I promise. It knows you're destined to be an acupuncturist, and Biology A-level helps you massively in this transition.

And please don't freak out about this right now – though I know you are, even as you are reading this! But honestly, I've got you. I'm here for you. You are not alone. Even in those times where you feel most alone, I am holding you close to my heart, to our heart.

For you, my beautiful little Water Element, trusting all of that right now is a tall order, it's scary, and I know that you can't see how to trust it right now and that's ok. For now, just trust ME. Trust the path I've walked for the last 20 years, the path I'm familiar with, the path I know you're trying to find right now. Try to trust that it will open up before you if you just put one foot slowly in front of the other.

My darling girl, it all turns out ok, in fact more than ok. It is wonderful - how can it not be wonderful, it is YOU we are talking about, or should I say you and me; we are one and the same. I so wish I could reassure you now in this tricky and uncertain phase of your life, but I know that even these powerful and prophetic words will only go part of the way... That's the beauty and challenge of Water.

Everything I am doing right now is because of all the hard work, insight, pain and growing you're doing now as a teenager. Thank you for sticking with it. Life now is amazing because you were strong enough, driven enough, and intuitive enough to walk the difficult path, the unusual path, the scary path – we are living this 'different' life now because of YOU, because you made the hard decisions and were so brave, even in the times you cried and wanted to give up, the times you wondered if it was all worth it, the times you couldn't trust it was all going to work out. Thank you, beautiful creature, you ARE doing it, it's ALL going to turn out ok. Trust the universe, trust me, and trust yourself. Trust us my love, and just keep going.

I love you xxx

What golden nuggets did you learn from this experience?

If I had known what it meant to be a Water Element person as a teenager, it would have saved so much heartache, so much soul searching, and so much pain. But the golden nuggets of understanding who I am, what I need, how I want to be in the world, came from the self-work I did back then, despite not having the Five Elements as my blueprint for self-understanding.

The therapy, the journaling, the endless reading of self-help books in my teens has made me who I am today. The fact that I am super emotional, highly sensitive, deeply feeling and an intense connector, makes me exceptionally good at my job. The emotions and turmoil I went through as a teenager was, in effect, the training ground for my vocation – for feeling all the feelings and being able to feel into other people's stuff. I just wish I had found the Five Elements earlier!

In the process of writing this letter to my younger self, I have realised just how much I would have benefitted from knowing that I was a Water Element personality type. It has really highlighted, exactly how much our Element shapes our motivations, our pain points, the wounds we carry, the stories we tell ourselves, how we feel about ourselves, and the overall narrative that runs in the background of our lives. All of these things may or may not be true or accurate, they are hugely coloured by our particular Element, and yet they form and guide important decisions about our lives and ourselves. This is why understanding which Element we are most influenced by is ultimately life-changing.

Would you have changed anything if you could go back?

As I completed my Advertising and Marketing Communications course less than a year before starting my acupuncture degree, many people often ask if I feel my original degree was a waste of time, or whether I would change my choice whilst at school applying for universities; I always say no.

It was my perfect, winding and destined path that led me to my life now. I could never have chosen the College of Integrated Chinese Medicine whilst I was choosing my A-levels and applying to universities as I had not even had acupuncture as a patient yet, and I was still utterly terrified of needles! Yes, an acupuncturist who was needle-phobic, and still is with hypodermic needles!

I honestly would not change a thing on my journey to this point. My two degrees now sit seamlessly alongside each other, creating an amazing business that does good things in the world, helping people towards health and happiness, giving them permission to just be themselves.

What would you tell other women who might be experiencing this in their lives?

For anyone who feels that they are broken or damaged, too sensitive or too emotional, I want you to know you are not. You are just you, and that is ok. You are your particular Element type and that is ok.

If you feel there is something wrong with you, that you are too different to other people, or if you are made to feel that your emotions are wrong, or what you want from your life is somehow too weird or unusual, I want you to know that there is absolutely nothing wrong with you. You CAN feel your feelings, in their fullest technicolour, without apology or making yourself small.

Even if you are different to absolutely everyone else in your life, it's ok. You do not need fixing. You do not need to be the same as them. You do not need to feel the same feelings that they do. Nor do you need to hide, avoid or squash down your feelings because they are too big or too intense. You do not need to apologise for feeling your feelings.

You don't need to have the same priorities as your family or friends, you don't need to tackle things in the same way that they do, or live like them. You are not 'wrong'. You may just be a different Element type to them, and that is ok. It's more than ok, I promise. It is beautiful and empowering and positive. Once you can understand yourself on this deep, gorgeous level, you can use your Element's gifts to live your absolute best, most fulfilling life. I will be standing next to you, holding space for you and cheering you on, so that you can embrace YOU, embrace your differences, embrace your beauty, and embrace your Element.

Sending so much goodness to you,

Rhiannon x

Any final words?

"Understanding yourself through the lens of the Five Elements, allows you to breathe a sigh of relief, and gives you permission to be your truest self."

Rhiannon Griffiths

How can people get in touch with you and see the work you do?

Website - www.rhiannongriffiths.com
Instagram - @rg_acupuncture
Facebook - fb.com/RhiannonGriffithsAcupuncture
Twitter - @rg_acupuncture

The Freedom to Do What I Want

Deenita Pattni: International trainer, speaker, author, and professional speaking coach.

What are you passionate about and how you are contributing to the world?

I am the founder of The Mind Vehicle Ltd, & Viamii, a training and development company helping individuals live and recognise the true potential inside them. My big "WHY" is to help these professionals overcome their limiting beliefs and feel empowered and encouraged to reach the business success they dream of by ongoing investment and development in themselves.

This mission has seen me speak on stages around the world including Europe, Australia, South Africa, Singapore to name but a few, sharing my knowledge and know-how with others.

Describe a pivotal time in your life you would like to share.

Have you ever asked yourself the question, "Why me?", or whispered, "If only...". Have you ever wished you could turn back the clock and change things, undo something you did, take the opportunity you missed?

There was a time in my life where I would have kept on asking myself the above questions and stayed stuck, lacking in confidence, feeling scared, and my blood flowing with traces of guilt, sadness, fear, obligation, rejection, anger, blame and self-pity.

It is Steve Jobs who said, "You can't connect the dots looking forward; you can only connect them looking backwards." I couldn't agree more as I look back; I can totally attribute where I am based on the decisions I made in the past which clearly made me stronger and the person I am today.

There are other pivotal points in my life, however, I felt the one I am about to describe was a crucial one. This event took my life, as I knew it, in a different direction. A world of unknowns and uncertainty. My parents made decisions during this period which they felt were right to protect me.

Only looking back can I see how these decisions potentially installed some limiting beliefs and insecurities within my unconscious.

If only I had been there to tell my younger self what she would be in store for. If only I had a looking glass into the future, so my younger self could see the light. If only I had a time machine. Come with me and experience this journey back in time and witness the words I would share with my younger self knowing what I know now.

Based on the wealth of knowledge, wisdom and experience that you have now, what would you have liked to say to yourself back then?

It's 1984; if you were with me, you'd be next to me as we walk down the corridor which leads us to a room in Dartford Hospital in Kent. As we enter the room, we cross paths with the doctor that has just been speaking to Deenita who's sat on the bed with tears running down her face. She's just been told she has diabetes and will need to take insulin for the rest of her life via daily injections. Injections she will need to learn to administer herself.

As I approach 12-year-old Deenita, I introduce myself. "Hi Deenita." As she looks up, I can see the worry and fear in her face. I can also see the same worry and fear in her mum's face; my mum's face. If you had met my mum, you would have met a lady who has unconditional love for those she cares about. A lady with a pure heart and exactly who you need by your side when all you want is a hug. Only if you knew my mum you would also know that she always thinks of the worst and I can see this in her face now. "Deenita, I know what you're feeling right now. Why? I felt the same. But that's why I am here."

I sit next to her on the bed and put my arm around her.

"Who are you?" she asks as she looks at me, comfortable but confused.

I smile at her, "I am here to tell you that everything is going to be OK. It's scary being in hospital, being told that you will now have to live a life where you'll have to take injections daily, miss out on your favourite sweets, watch

"The fears and insecurities are in your mind and have no basis for the truth. Life will throw some scary and challenging events at you every now and again. It's how you deal with and respond to them that will see you through to the other side."

-Deenita Pattni-

what you eat and drink, put a pin into your finger four times a day so you can test your blood sugars. All of it is a lot to take in and you're only 12.
"I don't understand. I don't get it. Was it all those fizzy drinks I had? Will I have to take injections every day? Do I have to take them myself? Will I be able to eat ice-cream? And why do I have to stay here away from my mum and dad and my brothers! Why can't I go home?"

(Funny the types of concerns a 12-year-old has, right?). But to a 12-year-old, these concerns feel like a huge weight. Their state of confusion lies around their life at the time.

"Deenita, despite everything you have heard, I promise you, it is not the end of the world. Only right now, it probably feels like it is."

As I heard my younger self, it took me right back there...

My mum and dad had driven me to a friend of theirs 60 miles from where we lived because they were deeply worried about me. The local GP, Dr Timmins – although a sweet old man, hadn't reacted fast enough for them. In their eyes, their daughter was looking more and more gaunt each day, exhausted and had been losing weight drastically.

As we arrived at Dr Patel's clinic in Dartford, Kent, not a moment was spared as they immediately took me to the nearest hospital where I was diagnosed with Type 1 diabetes and admitted straight away. I discovered a few hours later that, had I not been admitted that day, I was only a few days away from going into a diabetic coma.

The consultant who saw me in the hospital was kind and gentle. I remember liking him as he was very friendly. Only I couldn't stop the tears when he demonstrated how I would need to take injections twice a day for the rest of my life. As the day turned into evening, visiting hours were coming to an end and it was time for my mum and dad to leave. I knew we were far away from home and I felt alone, like I was being left there...

At this point, I could see the younger me. She wasn't worried about the diagnosis. She was just sad that she was being left on her own. It was at this point, I knew the words I would have liked to have heard:

"Hey Deenita..."

The younger me looked up, scared, anxious and upset.

"I know you're scared and I know at the moment, it feels like you're alone. I'm here to tell you that you will never be or feel alone. You have Mum and Dad; they love you and they'll be here every day. They won't miss a single drive to come and see you. They will always love you like you're their precious diamond in the rough. Your relationship with them will be one in a million and one which leads directly – heart to heart. And when you're faced with challenges in your life – and there will be a few along the way – it's your mum and dad's love, strength and values which will always help you through it. Each time you need them, they will both be there. They'll encourage you, drive you and support you and they will always be there for you."

I could see the younger Deenita looking confused as she looked up at me. "How do you know all this...who are you?"

"I know this because I am YOU. I've come to tell you just how amazing your life will be. You are destined to become an amazing and inspiring lady.

You'll be challenged for sure. You'll set yourself goals, and although they won't always lead you to what you think you should be doing, they'll lead you to bigger and better things. You'll fail and believe you're not good enough. You'll cry and then get right back up and try again. And this willpower, Deenita, you get from Dad – you'll never give up".

There is something very important you should know. Because of the amazing, confident, ambitious girl you will turn out to be, you'll help others feel and do the same. Just by being you, and giving and making time for others, you will influence so many to be able to realise their true potential. You will change their beliefs and behaviours and help them break through their blocks by simply being you – a beautiful woman with a giving heart.

I just want you to know that it won't be easy, because as you go into your teens and beyond, you'll believe your diabetes is a nuisance; it's in the way and you'll neglect it. You'll want to be like all your friends and not have to worry about when you eat, what you eat, and timings for your injections will become a last priority. You'll even miss appointments all because you want to feel like everyone else.

Here's the good news. It will not stop you from leading a normal life. Will you have to take some considerations into account? Sure, but it won't stop you from doing anything you want in life. You'll be able to travel all over the world, play sports, enjoy different cuisine.

And here's something you should remember: you don't want to be normal. You want to be exceptional, unique, and stand out. When you learn that being 'different' is amazing, you can achieve whatever you want in life, and you will. So, don't try to be ordinary – be extraordinary so your story can inspire others."

"Wow! That sounds like an amazing life. Will all that really happen?"

"Yes, Deenita, it will. And by the way – most people will call you Dee – and believe me, so many people will know who Dee is!

But I do want to spend a moment or two just letting you know the journey you will take in becoming me. What I am about to tell you is important because life won't be easy; you'll come across challenges and will want to take full responsibility for it; you'll feel like it's your job to make it OK or at times feel it's your fault. And this feeling of guilt and obligation will consume you...affecting your health and heart.

You give with all your heart for those you care about, and I want you to know that it's OK to give to yourself too. When those you love depart, leave, change or become distant, just know for however long they were in your life, they played a significant role and made you stronger. And you too served a purpose for them in more ways than you will ever know.

You will come across many people; some with whom you have a close bond, and some whose actions will cause you to believe that you can't do what you want to, you're not good enough, clever enough, or strong enough. Remember, you can be whomever and do whatever you want to; there is no stopping you and you must ensure you don't own other people's insecurities and limiting beliefs. When they try to give you their 'shit' – do not accept it. Let them own their shit and instead you continue to shine like the precious diamond you are.

Dee, stay focused on all the great there is because it's right in front of you. It's so easy to miss the good when you're focused on the bad! And the truth is, valuing all the good will ensure you captivate the best moments and, more importantly, capture the opportunities!

Finally, I just want to remind you of just how much you're loved. You have and will always have an amazing, extended family around you. Your mum and dad cherish you and are proud of what you have become; your brothers look up to you, even though they'll still tease you, and they'll always have your back, your cousins are inspired by you, and your nieces and nephews love you unconditionally. You are surrounded by friends who love your company and will be a part of your life for years to come – often reminding you of how amazing you are. You are a magnet and attract people to you wherever you go.

There is so much for you to look forward to. You will inspire and empower others and build a successful career for yourself. You will go on to build a business and do what you love – train others to become the best they can be. You will even become a published author (more than once) and you will grace stages all over the world training business professionals on how to be the best version of themselves. Opportunities will come to you because you are open to receiving them.

More importantly, you will learn to love you for you. And when you learn to love yourself and all that you have become, you will find LOVE.

As I left my younger self with those last words, I knew I had paved the path for her to face life with a smile knowing what she had to look forward to.

How did this event change your life?

As I look back, this event embedded in me a lot of insecurities that stayed for a long time. I always felt it restricted my life and that I lost the freedom to do what others could do without a second thought. From choosing to drink whatever I wanted all the way to just being able to be spontaneous without having to remember whether I had my medication with me or not.

I remember shortly after initially being diagnosed, my family made the decision to keep my condition a secret. Not because they were ashamed, but because my parents felt others would judge me. They'd see my condition as a long-term disease and think there was something wrong with me. I remember when I was 18 finding out that a guy who really liked me and wanted to marry me was told by his father that he would regret marrying someone with 'diabetes'.

It was these types of prejudices that scared my parents and they thought this would affect me finding love and happiness. However, after a relapse in my condition led me to being admitted into hospital, my parents and I made the decision that we would no longer keep it a secret. This was – if I was ever away from home and if anything happened, others would be able to help me. This understanding helped my parents to also feel secure. At the same time, I reminded them that what others thought of my condition didn't matter. If others misjudged me then that was their problem.

What golden nuggets did I learn from this experience?

At the time, you never realise the nuggets that are there during the experience – only after the fact. I learned that I was a lot stronger in dealing with challenging situations than I gave myself credit for, and that I adapted to living with a condition which I never used as an excuse not to do something.

I remember, in 2004, arriving at my very first motivational Personal Development event with Andy Harrington. Fire Your Desire. As I registered, I had to sign a waiver form to absolve the company of any responsibility should I be injured during the fire walk. My first reaction was to ask for an ambulance because 'I'm diabetic' and the lady behind the desk told me in no uncertain terms that there was no need for an ambulance. It was all about my intention!

She was right. I did the fire walk, a board-break, and bent a steel bar with my throat. And, in years to follow, I continued to do all of the above several times as well as a glass walk. Anything was possible.

I was lucky enough to have the right people around me as well as find the world of Personal Development to help me overcome my limiting beliefs which being diagnosed as a diabetic initially installed in me. Immersing and training myself in NLP gave me a new perspective and led to me overcoming fears and insecurities that I had adopted and unnecessarily owned.

I discovered that life's experiences are there for a reason. When you experience a significant event in your life – good or bad – there's definitely learning for you to take away. If you miss it, you wasted the experience. And I realised that everything I felt as a 12-year-old, the fears and anxieties I went through then, and months and years after, were there to protect me until I was ready to find the answers. For me, if I hadn't gone through this journey, I wouldn't have made the decisions and choices I did, and I wouldn't have achieved what I have today.

What would you tell someone else experiencing something similar?

The fears and insecurities are in your mind and have no basis for the truth. Life will throw some scary and challenging events at you every now and again. It's how you deal with and respond to them that will see you through to the other side. And if you're a parent whose child has been diagnosed with a condition, a condition they don't understand, ensure your fears and anxieties around it are not relayed unintentionally to them. As parents, I know from what my parents went through and decisions they made came from the right place. Except their fears became mine.

Would you have changed anything if you could go back?

Every experience I went through led me to where I am today and made me the person I am. Although I know I can't go back and share with my younger self all that I know now, I wouldn't change a thing.

Any final words?

"It's only in looking back that all the pieces, including the detours, fit together with wonderful logic."
Jean Chatzky

How can people get in contact?

Today, I live an incredible life. I started my business in 2012, a week before my 40th birthday, because I knew that I wanted to live a life doing what I love and have the time to spend with those close to me. As a single, strong and extraordinary woman, I also wanted to give myself time to find LOVE in my life so am on a journey to build a business which will continue to work without me having to exchange time.

Viamii Training Academy helps business professionals and recruitment experts market themselves as the go-to expert in their industry through personalised training programmes.

More information can be found at www.viamii.com or by emailing me at Deenita@viamii.com.

The Power of a Song

Tracy Leonetti, The French Connector.

What are you passionate about and how you are contributing to the world?

When I came to France over 25 years ago to live my dream, I struggled my way through the complex, and often intimidating, processes. There was no one to help me and I realised that it shouldn't be that difficult, so I created my business to help others integrate into the French life.

I really believe that when you are provided with the best information resources and support, your experience can only be enhanced, and that is why I'm building a network of the best specialists for people who want a seamless transition when starting a new life in the south of France and I'm doing this by providing people with the most current and up-to-date information, resources & support. This helps to save time and energy, and ultimately speeding up their integration into the French system so they can really live their dream life in France.

Describe a pivotal time in your life you would like to share:

Coming from a tough childhood in the 70s in Yorkshire, England, the middle child of three girls, at the age of seven it was often difficult to be heard, and quite frankly it felt that no one really wanted to listen, so I would just let everything happen around me and daydream about faraway places (yes, it started that early)! Each night in bed, I would pray first and then dream about where I could go when I was 'grown up'. It was often easier than living with the reality.

As three girls with very different characters, we were all put into categories growing up. The general consensus was that Tracy would be ok and I would always get by. In comparison to the labels given to my sisters, this was considered a good 'label' but nobody really wants to be labelled! So, I just kept my head down and got on with what needed doing at home and tried not to make any waves. I was extremely shy and reserved, which is hard to believe now if you ever met me, but yes, I would blush if anyone spoke to me.

I never really felt I had a voice at home, so I just loved going to school as that is where I felt I existed, it was where I escaped to. School for me was paradise!

Despite all of this, I've always felt special. I've always known deep down in my heart that I could achieve whatever I wanted. I never really understood why I felt this way and if you ask my elder sister, I'm sure she would say the same. I understood later on in life that this stemmed from a special song my mum used to sing to me when I was a child.

There were good and bad childhood memories. Some of my good childhood memories of holidays at Primrose Valley and Withernsea, discovering presents under the Christmas tree and playing cards with mum in front of the fire, are interspersed with periods of sadness, fear, guilt and sheer desperation at times because my mum suffered from an invisible illness—mental illness. Nowadays, it's commonly recognised as bipolar disorder. It's an incurable mental illness and its symptoms are periods of deep depression followed by periods of extreme highs.

My childhood, and that of my two sisters, was a rollercoaster ride of emotions due to mum's illness. Back in the 1970s, mental illnesses were hardly recognised and definitely not to be talked about for fear of what people would say or think. Dad tried desperately to manage us and look after Mum, but the side effects of the medication was often radical and dehumanising which would affect mum's personality, becoming either over excitable or a walking zombie.

Trying to make sense of the changes was very difficult as a small child. I didn't really understand what was happening, only that mum had good days and bad days. How I loved the good days, singing songs on the buses and playing games. I had difficulty understanding the bad days; it was just best to keep out of the way. Hospitalisations were frequent and unpleasant both for the patient and for the family. The hospitals were almost jail-like and as small children we had to go with her. Managing mum's medication was crucial to keep her stable, but she would often mistake her medication, I'm sure in attempt to reduce the debilitating side effects and it would, more often than not, result in a severe depression and hospitalisation.

" Everyone comes with their life baggage. We all have pasts, some better than others, some worse. Let that baggage work to your advantage, but don't let it determine who you are. "

-Tracy Leonetti-

I think one of the key pivotal experiences that is anchored in my memory is when my elder sister and I decided we had had enough and we were leaving home. Mum was in a particularly bad phase and dad just wasn't around when needed. He was a full-time worker and carer and was also trying to deal with his own demons.

I must have been about ten years old and my sister was twelve when we decided that it was time to leave home. The plan was not very adventurous - this was not one of the famous five adventures! We just knew we had to leave; it was a matter of survival. So, we packed a sandwich and off we went to one of our aunties. She said we couldn't stay but she gave us some money to get a bus to another aunty who said we could stay.

Of course, our father was promptly informed, and he came to see us. We were given a week's 'break' and then dad told us that mum really needed us and should go home. She was lost without us and promised that things would change. I had heard this statement a thousand times before. The choice was going home to mum 'who was doing much better now' or going to Cumbria to stay with another aunt. My elder sister, wisely, chose to leave but I felt the burden of guilt for leaving my mum and youngest sister who was only five at the time, so I went back. Who would look after them if we both went to Cumbria? In hindsight, not a problem a 10-year-old should need to deal with, and certainly not a situation that a father should put their child back into.

Looking back, what made it such an important part of your life journey?

Choices that are made when we are young impact us for years and the choice that I made to go back to mum, despite all that I had endured, instead of joining my sister in a safe haven in Cumbria, was life changing. Up until this ripe old age of ten I had been the middle sister but now the roles were changed. Instead of keeping my head down, I had to step up and protect and care for my younger sister, so I took on the role of parent to my younger sister, and carer for my mum. Dad nipped in and out of this environment but was never a permanent presence. He worked a lot, of course, but I always wondered where he went when he wasn't working.

What surprised me was how wonderful it felt to be needed and to actually be able to help. I was no longer invisible, and it wasn't all bad. Yes, there was a lot of responsibility but that helped me grow and learn quickly. On mum's good days we would have so much fun and she was like 'the mum I used to have'. When I was very young, my mum gifted me with my special song and it was during the good times that we would sing along to my song. We would also stay up late and listen to music. She often wanted me to stay off school with her, but I wouldn't do this, school was still my haven. Much later I realised that these were all symptoms of her illness!

This difficult period of my life helped me understand that I was special, strong and extremely capable, a gift that I will always be grateful for. In later years, finding my role in the family was difficult as I subconsciously yo-yoed between two roles, one being the middle sister and being the arbitrator of the family, and the elder sister who was the protector and carer. I lost myself for a long time whilst I struggled with my different roles.

Based on the wealth of knowledge, wisdom and experience that you have now, what would you have liked to say to yourself back then?

Dear Tracy,

One of your first memories that comes to mind is when you are about two years old. You are crying frantically in a strange place waiting for your mum to come and get you from your cot. This is not an ordinary cot, this is a hospital cot in a hospital dormitory. You and your elder sister are hospitalised with your mum and you are waiting for your mum to come and get you. One by one the mums come, but yours doesn't. Don't be scared Tracy, you have a protector. Your elder sister will climb over the cots and get into bed with you to keep you calm. Your elder sister, at the age of 4, had her role well in place at such a small age; protector and carer, one that she carries even today.

Later, when you lie in your bed each night praying for things to get better, know that they will. Know that you are going to have a wonderful life and you will fulfil the dreams that you have. But then, you always knew they would, didn't you?

When you are very young, you will often feel invisible, but when your mum sings your special song, "You are my special angel, sent from up above, the Lord smiled down on me and sent me an angel to love," know that this is her way of showing you that you are special, and although she couldn't always be there for you, or even be with you, your bond has been and always will be strong. You will find forgiveness easy for your mum, after all, she was ill. It will be more difficult for your dad.

You have to make some choices when you are very young, choices that a 12-year-old should not have to make. So, when your dad shows up with a van and is about to leave you alone with your mum and sister again, don't feel guilty that you had to beg him to take you with him, don't feel guilty that he would only take you, and don't feel guilty that you left your mum again. You have already given so much to your family, now is the time to become a child again. You didn't understand the situation and you were trying to survive. Forgive yourself and accept it. You will feel anger towards your dad for making you beg, for leaving your sister, for leaving your mum. Remember, he was just trying to cope with something for which he had no tools, experience or support and finally gave up. You are allowed to give up too. Know that you will go back and enjoy good times with your mum and your relationship will always be special. Your mum is a survivor and she will prove that time and time again over the years. That feeling you have of being special, even when times are tough, it comes from your mum. Hold it and cherish it and pass it on to your children. Despite your mum being ill all of her life, she is a fighter, and she will never give up.

As you go along your path, remember that you are not alone and that raising your hand and asking for support or help is neither a sign of weakness nor a sign of incapacity, it's a sign of acceptance of who you are. Don't hesitate, raise that hand! I know it's hard; you like to keep the peace and there is nothing wrong with being the arbitrator on occasion, but there will be situations when you will need to use your voice and speak out.

When your father walks into your room in later years and tells you not to go into higher education because you won't succeed, remember where he comes from. Remember his background, remember he is just trying to protect you. You are the first one to reject what he considers the 'normal' way of doing things. You are the first one to live with your boyfriend, the first one to reject getting married at 19. You are the first one who goes onto higher education after school and you are definitely the first one who wants to travel. Keep on your path, you can do it and you know it. He had difficulty protecting you very young, so he feels he needs to protect you as you get older. Embrace it rather than react to it.

When your opportunity to travel comes, you will hesitate because of the needs of your younger sister. She is still only a teenager and struggling. You feel you want to stay and protect her, but this is not your role. You will also hesitate because you have what everyone considers to be the dream job working for the civil service in Hull and, more importantly, you will hesitate because your mum needs you. You will feel torn inside. You are still in the role of carer and protector. Finally, your dad will step up and say,

"Go do it, Tracy." Go ahead and sever those ties and set off in pursuit of a new adventure to those faraway places that you dreamed of: Australia, New Zealand, Bermuda. This will help your younger sister become more independent and help your mum become stronger.

You will feel a lot of anger towards your father in your later years and even a little towards your elder sister. You felt alone and abandoned on many occasions, and you will struggle with forgiveness but learn to forgive and accept. Your elder sister was just a child, like you! She had been put in the role of protector from the first time you were in hospital with your mum at the age of two and that continued through many difficult situations in your early childhood. She also should not have had to make such a choice.

Embrace her and just be there for her when she needs you as she tries to change her role also. That is her personal struggle and you cannot help her with it, you can only be there to listen if she wants to talk. When you have children of your own it will become easier to forgive, and the olive branch that you hold out to your father will be accepted and a new relationship will begin; one filled with acceptance and love.

One of your most difficult combats will be establishing the correct roles with your younger sister. Having the role of a parent for most of her childhood and her teenage years will make it difficult for her to understand why you

204

cannot always be available for her. Why she cannot demand your help her in any given situation, at any time of the day or night. This will cause a lot of suffering for you and for her but it's a necessary pain as your role needs to be that of a sister, not of a carer or a protector. Persevere because one day she will understand, and then your relationship will be on an equal basis and you will share moments of pleasure, fun and complicity. It takes time, but anything worth having is worth waiting for!

Yes, you are a capable young lady with a feisty and passionate character and you can and will succeed, but don't feel that you have to prove it continually. You often feel like a square peg in a round hole. That's normal. You are different and will celebrate that difference as you get older. Helping people to obtain their dream lives will become your passion. Helping people take a step in the right direction, whatever that direction is, is essential to you. That feeling of being needed stays with you, but you can put it to good use in your professional life.

Over the years, in an attempt to be heard, you will stop listening and sometimes for fear of speaking out you will not ask those important questions. Be courageous and when a statement is made that you don't understand or don't agree with, ask the questions that are burning in your heart. Listen to the feedback. Take the time to absorb the information and learn from it without reacting. This will be a constant battle for you but persevere as this will be important for your children. Your children are a reflection of who you are, and in an effort to improve their lives you will 'dilute' your past. Share your past with them, be proud of who you are and where you come from and show them that they can achieve their dreams because they want to, not because they feel they need to and certainly not because they want to compare with you. Make sure they know that you are proud of them no matter they do. Your children will be your beacon and help you move forward.

Lastly, my dear Tracy, enjoy the life you build for yourself and your family. You made it happen, but you need to savour it. Don't measure yourself by other people's successes, only by your own and enjoy it.

Lots of love and hugs,
Tracy Xxx

How did this event change your life?

I believe that everyone, no matter what their role, is important. I sincerely believe that we are on an equal basis, from the assistant to the CEO.

My dream became a reality because I believed deep inside that if you really want something badly enough, you will make it happen. You may need help, you may need lots of time and patience, but you will get there. This positive thinking helped me knock down many obstacles in my past and keep moving forward.

What golden nuggets did you learn from this experience?

That it's not because you are capable of doing something that you should do it, or need to do it. That asking for help is not a sign of weakness. That forgiveness starts with yourself. That if you really want to achieve your goals for the right reasons, you will.

Ask questions when you don't understand a situation. This will avoid you drawing the wrong conclusions.

What would you tell other women who might be experiencing this in their lives?

Everyone comes with their life baggage. We all have pasts, some better than others, some worse. Let that baggage work to your advantage, but don't let it determine who you are. I truly believe that you can do and achieve anything, and I truly believe that you can achieve what you want if you really want it badly enough. However, I also believe that it should be done for the right reasons. You need to surround yourself with the right people who can provide the necessary support and encouragement to make that dream come true. Your dream doesn't have to be huge and world-changing; it does have to be something you care about.

Accept who you are. If you don't accept yourself, it will be difficult for others to do it.

Ensure that you raise your hand now again and ask for that help, whether it be to your partner, your children or a friend or an outsource.

Whoever it is that can help you down your path, go for it. Invest in your dream. Say no if you need to. Don't settle for second best and strive for your dreams. Whatever that dream is, take a baby step towards it each day and it will happen.
If I can do it, so can you!

Any final words?

My path has been formed by a series of pivotal moments, not just one. Each and every one of these experiences, often difficult at the time, formed the person I became today. Each and every one of them are held very tightly close to my heart as they involve all of my family members that I love dearly.

My story up until this point stems from my dreaming of faraway places as a small child but you need to know that the dream was the easy part. It was the dreaming and the visualisation that helped me survive some difficult times, however, making that dream happen was much more complicated. It took a lot of time, patience, experience, passion and drive.

I have now been able to transform my life experience into this positive energy and passion to help my customers with their challenges of creating a dream life in France. I simply Make It Happen.

It would be a pleasure to help anyone who is thinking of moving to France to connect with the right people or get the advice they need to help them decide if this is where they really want to be. It wasn't an easy dream all those years ago, as the red tape in France is complicated, so if your dream is to move to France, don't hesitate, contact me!

How can people get in touch with you and see the work you do? (insert links)

tracy@lbsinfrance.com
www.lbsinfrance.com
www.lbsinfrance.com/relocation

The Show Stopper

Tina Fotherby, founder of PR firm, Famous Publicity Ltd.

What are you passionate about and how you are contributing to the world?

I am passionate about making a positive contribution to society and raising the profile of great businesses and individuals who are doing brilliant work in helping others and making the world that one bit better, one moment at a time. I employ a team of seven in Surrey, near London, who work together in a friendly environment, delivering great results for their clients.

Describe a pivotal time in your life that you would like to share:

Aged 50, feeling the best I'd felt in a long time, and although not into fitness, I was planning to take part in a Tough Mudder mud run and was diagnosed with an advanced stage of breast cancer that needed immediate treatment.

I felt disorientated and found it very difficult to concentrate. I was in a state of shock but wanted to be as calm as possible. I found out through a phone call from my soon-to-be surgeon when I was returning home from work. The test taken the day before had shown that the tumour I had was aggressive and malignant. I felt terrible that by sharing my news I was hurting those who I loved most.

I told my husband (we'd been married 27 years at that point) the situation on arriving home and we were calm and quiet. There were no tears either side. We told the children once I knew the timing for the surgery, which luckily for me was just days away. The tumour was 43mm, the size of the face of a men's Tag Heuer watch, so there was much effort from my surgeon for quick action.

I told my teenage children about the illness and that I'd have surgery and be fine, which for most of the time over the next couple of years was my true belief. I knew that if I was strong, that they would respond in a positive way, which they did. I'm very glad to say that there were not visible public tears then either.

Calling my parents – who have been divorced for many years – with news of my diagnosis and the impending surgery, was very difficult and two of the toughest conversations.

What made things easier for me was the amazing support I received from my colleagues at work, not least my high-profile chairman and CEO for the well-known company I worked for, who were kind beyond belief. Also, both their wives were incredibly thoughtful and supportive, making me feel blessed to know such lovely individuals. My friends were brilliant too and offered me more support than I needed.

Looking back, what made it such an important part of your life journey?

It was an important part of my life journey because I realised the fragility of life but also my own strength. I knew that I was in control of my emotions and that if I chose to fall apart that would be totally unresourceful for those around me.

I realised that my own actions had an immediate effect on those close to me. Resilience breeds resilience.

It also made me think that there is so much more I want to do with my life; I won't let an illness get in the way.

Things I thought important as a child – love, being content, the company of friends and family, having fun, playing in woods, splashing in puddles and loving nature – all came flooding back to me.

Based on the wealth of knowledge, wisdom and experience that you have now, what would you have liked to say to yourself back then?

Dear Tina
I'm sending this message to you shortly before you received a diagnosis that would change you into being seriously grown up overnight.

Those crippling headaches you had a few months ago which pulsated in three-minute intervals, feeling like a metal band tightening around the crown of your head, were signals that all was not well. Such tension should not last for weeks and you've been lucky enough to be headache-free in the past.

The heat blasting from your body as you tried to sleep was not the menopause. It was a symptom of something far less 'natural'.
You will soon speak to a medical consultant and ask her, "Is it normal for someone who's never been ill and feeling really fit and well to have breast cancer?" and she will say, kindly and undramatically, "Yes, it happens every day."

You are likely to feel guilty that for some time before you visited your doctor you had suspicions that something was seriously wrong but pushed it to the back of your mind. This is partly because you have had previous experiences of benign problems that had sent you spinning. You will discover that women with a history of benign symptoms are at high risk, but you thought the opposite. You will also become terrified of 'unleashing a monster' so will delay visiting the doctor because you know that if the news is bad, the skies will darken, and all hell will break loose.
You've never liked drama queens. This is why you will attend every appointment and every treatment session alone, so as not to involve others in your melodrama.

You will develop strategies to soften the blow of distress. So, the first time you find it gross that you are shedding hair, you will shave your head completely and never have that problem again. You will embrace the wise woman in the quirky wig shop in Paddington who chose two fabulous wigs that will make you look more glamorous than ever. Only the hot weather will encourage you to remove these!

You will do really well to hold everything together at a very difficult time. You've never been very good at asking for help but there will be times in the future when you need to be better at accepting the gifts people give to you with their time.

Your experience will teach you the importance and value of precious moments. Had you not had the chance to stare metaphorically down the barrel of a gun, your values would be different. You are known for your impatience and in years to come you will be more careful about your use of time.

You will recover well from this set-back and in some ways, it will be the making of you, so long as you realise that you need to change areas of your thinking and being.

You will thank your friends who encouraged you to keep smiling and supported your idea of keeping a photo diary rather than a paper one, when you could not express your feelings.

At 30 you said you'd drunk your life's quota of champagne and, while you stopped bad habits when you were expecting your children, your wise young son will point out the relationship between alcohol and illness. Luckily, you will never be an alcoholic, although you will always be an addict of one kind or another and understand addictive behaviours. After all, addictions can be great distractions.

You will say that you will deal with your illness as best you can, with stoicism, and then forget about it. You will want to make something of your life after recovery, to show that such a traumatic event can be the beginning of something rather than the end.

As you've chosen a career in PR, you can never stand still because it's at the vanguard of constant change. But you will have the good fortune to work with some of the most interesting inventors, entrepreneurs and technical wizards of your generation. What's more, you will get to know many as good friends.

Yes, your illness will be a 'show-stopper' for a while, but if you listen to your closest colleagues you will know that it is good advice to come back to work, even if you're feeling dog rough. Why? Because then there will be no big drama about returning to work.

" Remember that we all die at some point. Now you've had a glimpse of that, make every day meaningful and don't even contemplate trivia. Embrace the big, important and expansive things going on and contribute to the power of love."

-Tina Fotherby-

You will realise that every day of your life will have a purpose, something that perhaps was forgotten.

You will learn that the 'power of love' is the strongest force that will be a huge source of energy and happiness.

You will be stopped in your tracks, but you will move forward, nurtured by the knowledge that you can change your mind and your beliefs. After this episode, you will love your body more than ever before and laugh about those who fear getting old! It's a privilege after all.

You used to be bemused by people who kept their illness a secret, but you will quickly learn that this is an incredibly useful strategy for many. Dealing with other people's reaction to your illness can be difficult.

You will grit your teeth — in five years' time when you have the all-clear — when an acquaintance will ask, "But are you really, really well?" and then discuss someone they've known who'd had a tragic second hit of the disease.

While up until now you've been sanguine and unphased by the passing of the lives of others, especially older people with a fulfilling life, you will be devastated when those who've been kind to you will move on to a different plane. Death suddenly seems a lot more personal.

How did this event change your life?

This event made me realise the importance of living in the present and enjoying every moment in full. While my work colleagues were fantastic, I had to move on afterwards and change my routine. The first thing to go was my long commute to London. I also wanted time to fine-tune my interpersonal skills. I wanted to tackle self-limiting beliefs so studied Neuro Linguistic Programming and hypnotherapy to a level high enough to deal with my mental incapacity that was a by-product of toxic chemotherapy.

What golden nuggets did you learn from this experience?

I learned to notice the absence of negative things and appreciate that. You only live once, so make the most of it! An epic ability to forget will hinder your cognitive abilities for a good couple of years, but it will be restored so long as you have an open mind and continue to learn. And being forgetful can be a good thing. I learned the stigma associated with cancer – whatever the type. My bond is with others touched by this condition.

What would you tell other women who might be experiencing this in their lives?

Visit the best website: https://www.macmillan.org.uk/, especially for its explanation of therapies. If you want to drive yourself nuts, surf the internet randomly for advice.

Be aware of the difficulties faced by colleagues and close family members, especially those who might feel that they are at risk. I was lucky because my age showed that I was not pre-disposed to the disease.

Know that you will be bombarded by ads for life assurance when using Gmail.

One of the toughest things is updating people on your medical status. It can be tedious. Go for a weekly or fortnightly email that's brief and informative. Screen your calls when you are tired.

Be more selfish. You've probably got this illness because you've put yourself at the back of the queue for too long.

Keep a journal or a photo record of your experience. I took lots of photos when I couldn't put my thoughts into words. Reviewing them now, I know that I'm in good shape, all things considered.

Enjoy make-up and its transformative power with the excitement of a teenager!

There are better life-changing experiences. The surgery was the easy bit. Chemo was debilitating, and radiotherapy is very tiring. (Luckily, I did not need the latter.)

Expect to be off work for several weeks (in my case, about ten) and be prepared to be under par for one to two years. Fresh air, exercise and learning new things will keep you stimulated.

Know that you can keep your illness private if you would like to. It's a bit of white lie but it saves you being pitied, which is my least favoured sentiment.

Would you have changed anything and, if so, what are some of the things you would have changed about that situation if you could have?

I would like to have known that it is not unusual to have a 'meltdown' about one to two years after diagnosis. In my desire to be resourceful, I avoided anything resembling self-help when it could have been very useful.

Any final words?

Remain fearless and be proud of that. Love the little things in life. Mix with people who uplift you. Note that you are fortunate when compared to others, for example, those who might want children and find themselves stopped in their tracks. Spot the kind things people do and thank them. Admit to your mistakes and know that to err is human. Forgive yourself for the upset you have undoubtedly caused to others. Remember that we all die at some point. Now you've had a glimpse of that, make every day meaningful and don't even contemplate trivia. Embrace the big, important and expansive things going on and contribute to the power of love.

How can people get in touch with you and see the work you do?

Website: http://www.famouspublicity.com/
Twitter: https://twitter.com/TinaFotherby
LinkedIn: https://www.linkedin.com/in/tina-fotherby-0466b54/

Write your own
'Note to My Younger Self'

I hope you have enjoyed reading all the inspirational stories within this book. The power of writing a "Note to Your Younger Self" and reviewing some of your darkest moments with fresh eyes to see the lessons learnt and the stepping stones these experiences have given provides hope, wisdom, inspiration and empowerment.

Here is your opportunity to write your own "Note to your younger self". Take the time to find a quiet space, where you will be undisturbed and ask yourself the following questions.

1.   Describe a pivotal moment in your life.

2.   Looking back what made it such an important part of your journey?

3.   Based on the wealth of knowledge, wisdom and experience that you

       now, what would you have liked to say to yourself back then?

4.   How did this event change your life?

5.   What golden nuggets did you learn from this experience?

6.   What would you tell other women who might be experiencing this in

       their lives?

7.   Would you have changed anything and, if so, what are some of the

       things you would have changed about that situation if you could have?

8.   How do you feel that this experience has contributed to discovering

       your true purpose and how you show up in the world?

To make it easier for you, I would love to share with you for free, my 'Map Your Past, To Create a Better Future' tool, which will help you map your past and decide which of your pivotal moments is the most important to write about. To download follow the link below.

https://womenofcontribution.lpages.co/the-pay-it-forward-series-notes-to-my-younger-self/

Once you have completed your story, why not head over to
www.facebook.com/groups/womenofcontribution

and tell us all about your experience.

Special Thanks

Thank you to the phenomenal women whose stories are written within these pages. Your understanding of my vision and the true power of what can be achieved when we come together in a single cause, a cause to make the world a better place for women around the world has been amazing. It has been a pleasure to work with each and every one of you.

A special thank you to Sammy Blindell for encouraging me to believe that I could bring this book to light and for guiding me through those moments of self-doubt, fear and worry and for designing the most perfect book cover a woman could ask for. Massive thank you to both Marie Diamond and Marci Shimoff for your unwavering endorsement of our book and message.
Thank you to Sally DiCesare and Shelley Chapman for your contribution too.

This book has always been about how I, and many others can serve the world, pay forward our gifts, our knowledge and shine our light. Surrounding myself with great women has allowed me to not only see the light that shines uniquely within me but to help others to shine theirs too as we come together to impact on 1 million lives.

Because united we are strong, together we can make a difference, one woman at a time.

Special Thanks

I want to say a very special thank you to Stewart Pearce, God certainly pulled out all the stops when he introduced you to me. I am truly humbled by your large and giving heart and your mission to help women see the magic within, you are a true man of contribution and I will be forever grateful that you came into my life.

For more information about Stewart and the fabulous work he does join both him and I on his phenomenal radio show www.thewayforward.org.uk which is aired on www.ukhealthradio.com

Our Chosen Charity

The Pay It Forward Series is proud to be supporting #MoveToEndDV.

Founded by Meathead Movers, a for-profit student athlete moving company that provides free moving services to victims of domestic violence, #MoveToEndDv's mission is to encourage 10,000 businesses all over the world to donate free products or services to shelters, victims and survivors of domestic violence. By connecting shelters and businesses all over the world, #MoveToEndDv aims to change the way communities respond to domestic violence situations, help victims and survivors to start a new life through comprehensive community support, and help put an end to abuse once and for all.

To discover more visit: https://movetoenddv.org

SPACE FOR NOTES

.